Qualifications and Credit Framework (QCF)
LEVEL 4 DIPLOMA IN ACCOUNTING

(QCF)

QUESTION BANK

Financial Performance

2011 Edition

First edition 2010

Second edition July 2011

ISBN 9780 7517 9767 1

(Previous edition 9780 7517 8605 7)

British Library Cataloguing-in-Publication Data
A catalogue record for this book is available from the British
Library

Published by

BPP Learning Media Ltd
BPP House
Aldine Place
London W12 8AA

www.bpp.com/learningmedia

Printed in the United Kingdom

CONTENTS

Introduction   (v)

Question and Answer bank

A NOTE ABOUT COPYRIGHT

INTRODUCTION

This is BPP Learning Media's AAT Question Bank for Financial Performance. It is part of a suite of ground-breaking resources produced by BPP Learning Media for the AAT's assessments under the qualification and credit framework.

The Financial Performance assessment is **computer assessed**. As well as being available in the traditional paper format, this **Question Bank is available in an online format** where all questions and assessments are presented in a **style which mimics the style of the AAT's assessments.** BPP Learning Media believe that the best way to practise for an online assessment is in an online environment. However, if you are unable to practise in the online environment you will find that all tasks in the paper Question Bank have been written in a style that is as close as possible to the style that you will be presented with in your online assessment.

This Question Bank has been written in conjunction with the BPP Text, and has been carefully designed to enable students to practise all of the learning outcomes and assessment criteria for the units that make up Financial Performance. It is fully up to date as at July 2011 and reflects both the AAT's unit guide and the specimen assessment provided by the AAT.

This Question Bank contains these key features:

- Tasks corresponding to each chapter of the Text. Some tasks are designed for learning purposes, others are of assessment standard

- The AAT's two specimen assessments and answers for Financial Performance

- Four further practice assessments

The emphasis in all tasks and assessments is on the practical application of the skills acquired.

If you have any comments about this book, please e-mail suedexter@bpp.com or write to Sue Dexter, Publishing Director, BPP Learning Media Ltd, BPP House, Aldine Place, London W12 8AA.

Question bank

Chapter 1

Task 1.1

At a production level of 16,000 units the production cost incurred totals £54,400. At a production level of 22,000 units the same cost totals £68,200.

This a variable cost. True or false? Tick the correct box.

True ☐

False ☐

Task 1.2

The following details are available for four types of costs at two activity levels:

Cost type	Cost at 1,000 units	Cost at 1,500 units
I	£7,000	£10,500
II	£11,000	£12,500
III	£12,000	£12,000
IV	£3,800	£5,700

Complete the table to classify each cost by behaviour:

Cost	Behaviour
Cost I	
Cost II	
Cost III	
Cost IV	

Task 1.3

A manufacturing business anticipates that its variable costs and fixed costs will be £32,000 and £25,000 respectively at a production level of 10,000 units.

Complete the table to show the total production cost and the cost per unit at each of the activity levels.

Activity level – units	Total production cost – £	Cost per unit – £
8,000		
12,000		
15,000		

Task 1.4

The costs of a supervisor at a manufacturing company are £20,000. One supervisor is required per 750 units produced.

Complete the table to show the total supervisors cost and the supervisors cost per unit at each of the activity levels.

Activity level – units	Total supervisors cost £	Supervisors cost per unit £
500		
1,000		
1,500		

Task 1.5

Given below are a number of types of cost – classify each one according to its behaviour:

		Cost behaviour
(i)	Maintenance department costs which are made up of £25,000 of salaries and an average of £500 cost per call out	
(ii)	Machinery depreciation based upon machine hours used	
(iii)	Salary costs of nursery school teachers, where one teacher is required for every six children in the nursery	
(iv)	Rent for a building that houses the factory, stores and maintenance departments	

Task 1.6

A business produces one product which requires the following inputs:

Direct materials	6 kg @ £4.80 per kg
Direct labour	4 hours @ £7.00 per hour
Building costs	£18,000 per quarter
Leased machines	£600 for every 500 units of production
Stores costs	£3,000 per quarter plus £3.00 per unit

(i) Complete the table to show the total cost of production and the cost per unit at each of the quarterly production levels.

Production level – units	Total cost of production £	Cost per unit £
1,000		
1,500		
2,000		

(ii) Explain why the cost per unit is different at each level of production.

....

Task 1.7

The costs of a factory maintenance department appear to be partially dependent upon the number of machine hours operated each month. The machine hours and the maintenance department costs for the last six months are given below:

	Machine hours	Maintenance cost £
June	14,200	285,000
July	14,800	293,000
August	15,200	300,000
September	14,500	290,000
October	15,000	298,000
November	14,700	292,000

The variable cost per machine hour is £ [   ]

The fixed costs of the maintenance department are £ [   ]

....

Task 1.8

The activity levels and related production costs for the last six months of 20X8 for a business have been as follows:

	Activity level	Production cost
	Units	£
July	63,000	608,000
August	70,000	642,000
September	76,000	699,000
October	73,000	677,000
November	71,000	652,000
December	68,000	623,000

(a) The fixed element of the production costs is £ [   ]

The variable element of the production costs per unit is £ [   ]

(b) Complete the table to show the estimated production costs at each of the levels of production.

Level of production – units	Production cost – £
74,000	
90,000	

(c) Comment upon which of the two estimates of production costs calculated in b) is likely to be most accurate and why.

Chapter 2

Task 2.1

The budgeted overheads of a manufacturing business have been allocated and apportioned to the two production cost centres as follows:

Cutting	£58,600
Finishing	£42,400

The two production cost centres are budgeted to produce 10,000 units in the next period.

You are also provided with the following further information:

	Cutting	Finishing
Direct labour hours	4,000	24,000
Machine hours	12,000	2,000
Direct labour cost	£24,500	£168,000
Direct materials cost	£180,000	£25,000
Prime cost	£204,500	£193,000

Complete the following table to calculate overhead absorption rates for each of the two production cost centres. Choose from the picklist when each absorption rate would be appropriate.

Absorption rate method	Cutting rate £	Finishing rate £	Most appropriate 1, 2 or 3
Rate per unit			
Rate per direct labour hour			
Rate per machine hour			

Picklist

1 Most appropriate in a largely mechanised department where most of the overhead relates to machinery costs

2 Most appropriate where all products are of similar size and require a similar input in terms of time and resources of the departments

3 Most appropriate in labour intensive departments where most of the overhead relates to labour

Task 2.2

The budgeted overheads apportioned to a business's two production cost centres, C and D, together with the budgeted labour hours and machine hours, are given below:

	C	D
Overheads	£125,000	£180,000
Direct labour hours	12,000	80,000
Machine hours	100,000	10,000

Production cost centre C is a highly mechanised department with only a few machine operatives whereas production cost centre D is a highly labour intensive department.

(a) Complete the table to calculate separate departmental overhead absorption rates for each production cost centre using an appropriate basis.

Department	Overhead absorption rate £
C	
D	

(b) Each unit of Product P spends the following hours in each production department:

	C	D
Direct labour hours	1	7
Machine hours	5	2

The overhead to be included in the cost of each unit of product P is £ [   ]

Task 2.3

In each of the following situations calculate any under- or over-absorption of overheads and state whether this would be a debit or a credit in the income statement (profit and loss account):

	Under-absorption £	Over-absorption £	Debit/Credit
Budgeted production was 1,200 units and budgeted overheads were £5,400. Overheads are to be absorbed on a unit basis. The actual production was 1,000 units and the overheads incurred were £5,000.			
Budgeted production was 600 units to be produced in 1,800 labour hours. Budgeted overheads of £5,040 are to be absorbed on a direct labour hour basis. The actual production for the period was 700 units in 2,200 labour hours and the actual overheads were £5,100.			
Budgeted production was 40,000 units and the budgeted machine hours were 2 hours per unit. Budgeted overheads were £320,000 and were to be absorbed on a machine hour basis. The actual overheads incurred were £320,000 and the production was 42,000 units. The total machine hours were 82,000.			

Task 2.4

A business produces a single product in its factory which has two production departments, cutting and finishing. In the following quarter it is anticipated that 120,000 units of the product will be produced. The expected costs are:

Direct materials	£12 per unit
Direct labour	2 hours cutting @ £7.40 per hour
	1 hour finishing @ £6.80 per hour
Variable overheads cutting	£336,000
finishing	£132,000
Fixed overheads cutting	£144,000
finishing	£96,000

Overheads are absorbed on the basis of direct labour hours.

The unit cost under absorption costing will be £ ▢

The unit cost under marginal costing will be £ ▢

....

Task 2.5

Given below are the budgeted production and sales figures for the single product that a business makes and sells for the months of July and August.

	July	August
Production	24,000 units	24,000 units
Sales	22,000 units	25,000 units

There was inventory (stock) of 1,500 units of the product at the start of July.

The expected production costs for each of the two months are as follows:

Direct materials	£6.80 per unit
Direct labour	£3.60 per unit
Variable production costs	£32,400
Fixed production costs	£44,400

Overheads are absorbed on the basis of the budgeted production level and the product is sold for £16 per unit.

(a) The absorption costing profit for July was £ ▢

The absorption costing profit for August was £ ▢

The marginal costing profit for July was £ ▢

The marginal costing profit for August was £ ▢

(b) Prepare a reconciliation explaining any difference in the two profit figures in each of the two months.

....

Task 2.6

You are given the budgeted data about the production of a business's single product for the following quarter:

Opening inventory (stock)	840 units
Production	8,000 units
Sales	8,200 units
Direct materials	£23.60
Direct labour	4 hours @ £5.80 per hour
Variable overheads	£88,000
Fixed overheads	£51,200

Overheads are absorbed on the basis of units of production. The product has a selling price of £70 per unit.

(a) The profit for the quarter under absorption costing is £ [   ]

The profit for the quarter under marginal costing is £ [   ]

(b) Prepare a reconciliation explaining any difference in the profit using absorption costing and profit using marginal costing.

....

Task 2.7

Charleroi Aircon Ltd design and install industrial air-conditioning systems. The company is based in Birmingham.

Charleroi's usual pricing policy is to use direct costs (equipment and installation labour) plus a mark-up of 50% to establish the selling price for an air-conditioning installation.

The company is about to tender for two contracts, quotation HMG/012 and quotation CFG/013.

The company is in the process of designing an Activity Based Costing system and the following information has been obtained about the two jobs.

Estimates related to contracts HMG/012 and CFG/013		
Contract number:	*HMG/012*	*CFG/013*
Equipment: cost	£175,000	£120,000
number of items purchased	650	410
Direct labour: hours	10,000	6,000
hourly rate	£13	£11
Design hours	1,280	620
Distance from Birmingham office (miles round-trip)	320	90
	30	10
Engineer site visits required		

The following overhead information is also available in relation to ABC costs.

ABC details for overhead activities connected with air conditioning installation contracts			
Activity	*Budgeted cost pool £pa*	*Cost driver*	*Cost driver units pa*
Design department	675,000	Design hours	25,000
Site engineers	370,000	Miles travelled	185,000
Purchasing department	105,000	Items purchased	15,000
Payroll department	75,000	Direct hours	300,000
Site management	750,000	Direct hours	300,000
Post-installation inspection	80,000	Items purchased	20,000

(a) **Usual pricing policy**

The price of job HMG/012 based upon direct costs plus 50% mark-up is £ [   ]

The price of job CFG/013 based upon direct costs plus 50% mark-up is £ [   ]

(b) Complete the tables to show the activity-based overhead costs for each of jobs HMG/012 and CFG/013.

Activity	Budgeted cost pool	Cost driver	Cost driver units pa	Cost per unit of cost driver
	£			£
Design department				
Site engineers				
Purchasing department				
Payroll department				
Site management				
Post-installation inspection				

Cost pool	Total Cost HMG/012	Total Cost CFG/013
	£	£
Design department		
Site engineers		
Purchasing department		
Payroll department		
Site management		
Post-installation inspection		
Total cost		

Task 2.8

You are employed as a financial analyst at Drampton plc, a computer retailer. Drampton plc has recently taken over Little Ltd, a small company making personal computers and servers. Little appears to make all of its profits from servers. Drampton's finance director tells you that Little's fixed overheads are currently charged to production using standard labour hours and gives you their standard cost of making PCs and servers. These are shown below.

Little Ltd: Standard cost per computer

Model	Server	PC
Annual budgeted volume	5	5,000
Unit standard cost		
	£	£
Material and labour	50,000	500
Fixed overhead	4,000	40
Standard cost per unit	54,000	540

The finance director asks for your help and suggests you reclassify the fixed overheads between the two models using activity-based costing. You are given the following information.

- **Budgeted total annual fixed overheads**

	£
Set-up costs	10,000
Rent and power (production area)	120,000
Rent (stores area)	50,000
Salaries of store issue staff	40,000
Total	220,000

Every time Little makes a server, it has to stop making PCs and rearrange the factory layout. The cost of this is shown as set-up costs. If the factory did not make any servers these costs would be eliminated.

- **Cost drivers**

	Server	PC	Total
Number of set-ups	5	0	5
Number of weeks of production	10	40	50
Floor area of stores (square metres)	400	400	800
Number of issues of inventory (stock)	2,000	8,000	10,000

Complete the table to show how to reallocate Little's budgeted total fixed annual overheads between server and PC production on an Activity Based Costing basis.

	Server allocated overheads £	PC allocated overheads £
Set-up costs		
Rent and power (production area)		
Rent (stores area)		
Salaries of stores issue staff		
Total overheads		

Task 2.9

You are the management accountant at a manufacturing company which makes two products, the Plastic and the Metal. Standard costing information for direct material and labour costs are given for the two products below.

Product	Plastic	Metal
Budgeted production units	5,000	1,000
Unit standard cost		
	£	£
Material	10	25
Labour	2	4

The company has the following budgeted overheads.

	£
Power for machinery	110,000
Rent of factory	120,000
Canteen costs	40,000
Total	270,000

The cost drivers for these costs are given below, for the different products.

- **Cost drivers**

	Plastic	Metal	Total
Machine hours	2,500	3,000	5,500
Floor space (square metres)	1,000	200	1,200
Number of employees	200	50	250

Complete the table to show how to reallocate the budgeted total overheads between the two products on an Activity Based Costing basis.

	Plastic allocated overheads £	Metal allocated overheads £
Power for machinery		
Rent of factory		
Canteen costs		
Total overheads		

Chapter 3

Task 3.1

A business sells a single product and has budgeted sales of 115,000 units for the next period. The selling price per unit is £28 and the variable costs of production are £17. The fixed costs of the business are £1,100,000.

The breakeven point in units is [   ] units

The margin of safety in units is [   ] units

The margin of safety as a percentage of budgeted sales is [   ]

∙∙∙

Task 3.2

The following information relates to one period for Product D which is manufactured by Mild Ltd.

Expected sales revenue = £160,000

Selling price per unit = £16 per unit

Variable cost = £8 per unit

Fixed costs = £40,000

The breakeven point both in terms of units and sales revenue is:

	Breakeven point in units	Breakeven point in sales revenue
A	5,000 units	£40,000
B	5,000 units	£80,000
C	10,000 units	£40,000
D	10,000 units	£80,000

∙∙∙

Task 3.3

The following information relates to one period for Product V which is manufactured by Hay-on-Wye Ltd.

Selling price per unit = £80

Variable cost per unit = £25

Budgeted fixed costs = £110,000

Budgeted sales = 2,500 units

The margin of safety, in terms of both units and sales revenue is:

	Units	Sales revenue
A	500	£12,500
B	2,000	£160,000
C	1,900	£152,000
D	500	£40,000

Task 3.4

A business sells a single product at a selling price of £83 and the variable costs of production and sales are £65 per unit. The fixed costs of the business are £540,000.

The number of units of the product that the business must sell in order to make a target profit of £300,000 is [   ] units.

Task 3.5

A business sells its single product for £40. The variable costs of this product total £28. The fixed costs of the business are £518,000.

The sales revenue required in order to make a target profit of £250,000 is £ [   ]

Task 3.6

Three products are produced by a business. There is a shortage of the material which is used to make each product, with only 3,000 kg available in the coming period.

	Product		
	A	B	C
Direct materials @ £4 per kg	£8	£4	£16
Direct labour @ £10 per hour	£20	£5	£15
Selling price	£40	£25	£47
Maximum sales demand	1,000 units	800 units	600 units

Complete the table to determine the production plan which will maximise contribution.

Product	Units

Task 3.7

A business produces three products. Production and sales details are given below:

	Product		
	R	S	T
Direct materials @ £5 per kg	£20	£25	£15
Direct labour @ £7 per hour	£14	£21	£21
Selling price	£45	£60	£55
Machine hours per unit	4	3	2
Maximum sales demand	20,000 units	25,000 units	8,000 units

During the next period the supply of materials is limited to 250,000 kgs, the labour hours available are 100,000 and the machine hours available are 180,000.

Complete the table to determine the production plan which will maximise contribution.

Product	Units

The contribution that will be earned under this production plan is £ [　　　　　　]

. . . .

Task 3.8

A company is considering the purchase of a small sole trader's business for a cost of £84,000 on 30 June 20X5. The estimated cash inflows from the purchased business are:

	£
30 June 20X6	26,000
30 June 20X7	30,000
30 June 20X8	21,000
30 June 20X9	14,000

Thereafter the purchased business will be closed down and its operations merged with the other operations of the company.

The company has a cost of capital of 7% and analyses potential investments using the net present value method.

The discount factors at 7% are as follows:

Year	Discount factor
0	1.000
1	0.935
2	0.873
3	0.816
4	0.763

The net present value of the investment is £ [   ]

....

Task 3.9

The managers of a business are considering investing in a new factory. It has been estimated that the cost now would total £355,000. The anticipated profit for the factory for each of the next five years are as follows:

	Profit
	£
Year 1	47,000
Year 2	55,000
Year 3	68,000
Year 4	53,000
Year 5	22,000

The profit figures given are after charging depreciation of £60,000 in each year. The business has a cost of capital of 12%.

The discount factors at 12% are as follows:

Year	Discount factor
0	1.000
1	0.893
2	0.797
3	0.712
4	0.635
5	0.567

The net present value of the potential investment is £ [   ]

....

Task 3.10

A company is to invest in a project with an immediate cash outflow of £200,000. The receipts from this project are £90,000 in one year's time, £130,000 in two years' time and finally £70,000 in three years' time.

The interest rate applicable to the company is 7%

Calculate the net terminal value of the project.

Chapter 4

Task 4.1

Given below are the production cost figures for the last ten months. Calculate a three month moving average for these figures.

	Production costs	Three month moving total	Three month moving average
	£	£	£
March	104,500		
April	110,300		
May	112,800		
June	109,400		
July	117,600		
August	116,000		
September	119,200		
October	122,300		
November	120,500		
December	119,300		

Task 4.2

A new restaurant has recently been opened which only trades for five days a week. The takings have been increasing rapidly over the first four weeks since opening, as given below.

Complete the table to calculate the five day moving average and the daily seasonal variations in accordance with the additive model.

		Actual	5-day Moving average – TREND	Seasonal variation (actual – trend)
		£	£	£
Week 1	Day 1	600		
	Day 2	700		
	Day 3	1,000		
	Day 4	1,200		
	Day 5	1,500		
Week 2	Day 1	680		
	Day 2	750		
	Day 3	1,250		
	Day 4	1,400		
	Day 5	1,860		
Week 3	Day 1	820		
	Day 2	1,030		
	Day 3	1,940		
	Day 4	2,100		
	Day 5	2,500		
Week 4	Day 1	1,000		
	Day 2	1,320		
	Day 3	1,560		
	Day 4	2,290		
	Day 5	2,670		

Task 4.3

Given below are the quarterly sales figures for a small business. Complete the table to calculate the trend using a four month centred moving average and the seasonal variations using the additive model.

		Actual	4-quarter moving average	Centred moving average – TREND	Seasonal variations
		£	£	£	£
20X5	Quarter 3	50,600			
	Quarter 4	52,800			
20X6	Quarter 1	55,600			
	Quarter 2	48,600			
	Quarter 3	51,200			
	Quarter 4	53,900			
20X7	Quarter 1	58,000			
	Quarter 2	49,800			
	Quarter 3	53,000			
	Quarter 4	54,600			
20X8	Quarter 1	60,100			
	Quarter 2	50,700			
	Quarter 3	54,200			
	Quarter 4	55,200			

Complete the following table to average the seasonal variations.

	Quarter 1	Quarter 2	Quarter 3	Quarter 4
	£	£	£	£
20X6				
20X7				
20X8				

Task 4.4

A business uses time series analysis and has found that the predicted trend of sales for the next four quarters and historical seasonal variations are as follows:

	Predicted trend	Seasonal variation
	£	£
Quarter 1	418,500	+21,500
Quarter 2	420,400	+30,400
Quarter 3	422,500	−16,700
Quarter 4	423,800	−35,200

What are the predicted actual sales figures for these four quarters?

Quarter 1

Quarter 2

Quarter 3

Quarter 4

Task 4.5

Given below are the production cost figures for a business and the Retail Price Index for the last six months.

(a) Complete the table to show the production cost figures in terms of January's prices.

	Actual costs	RPI	Workings	Costs at January prices
	£			£
January	129,600	171.1		
February	129,700	172.0		
March	130,400	172.2		
April	131,600	173.0		
May	130,500	174.1		
June	131,600	174.3		

(b) Complete the table to show the production cost figures in terms of June's prices.

	Actual costs	RPI	Workings	Costs at June prices
	£			£
January	129,600	171.1		
February	129,700	172.0		
March	130,400	172.2		
April	131,600	173.0		
May	130,500	174.1		
June	131,600	174.3		

Task 4.6

Given below are the quarterly sales figures for a business for the last two years. Complete the table in order to calculate an index for these sales with quarter 1 20X7 as the base period.

		Actual	Workings	Index
		£		
20X7	Quarter 1	126,500		
	Quarter 2	130,500		
	Quarter 3	131,400		
	Quarter 4	132,500		
20X8	Quarter 1	133,100		
	Quarter 2	135,600		
	Quarter 3	136,500		
	Quarter 4	137,100		

Task 4.7

AB Ltd set the standard cost of material C at £3.50 per litre when an index of material prices stood at 115. The index now stands at 145.

The updated standard cost for material C is £ [   ]

Task 4.8

The direct materials cost for quarter 1 and quarter 2 of next year have been estimated in terms of current prices at £657,000 and £692,500 respectively. The current price index for these materials is 126.4 and the price index is estimated as 128.4 for quarter 1 of next year and 131.9 for quarter 2.

What are the forecast direct materials costs for quarters 1 and 2 of next year?

Quarter 1 £ [   ]

Quarter 2 £ [   ]

Task 4.9

The total production cost varies linearly with the volume of production, and so can be described by the linear regression equation:

$$y = a + bx$$

where x is the volume of production.

If the total production cost of 100 units is £2,500, and the total production cost of 1,000 units is £7,000, what are the values of a and b?

a £ [   ]

b £ [   ]

The total production cost for 750 units is £ [   ]

··

Task 4.10

The linear regression equation for production costs for a business is:

$$y = 138,000 + 6.4x$$

where x is the number of units

If production is expected to be 105,000 units in the next quarter the anticipated production costs are £ [   ]

··

Task 4.11

The linear regression equation for the power costs of a factory is given as follows:

$$y = 80,000 + 0.5x$$

where x is the number of machine hours used in a period.

The anticipated machine hours for April are 380,000 hours.

The anticipated power costs for April are £ [   ]

··

Task 4.12

The linear regression equation for the trend of sales in thousands of units per month based upon time series analysis of the figures for the last two years is:

$$y = 3.1 + 0.9x$$

What is the estimated sales trend for each of the first three months of next year?

Month 1   [   ] units

Month 2   [   ] units

Month 3   [   ] units

··

Task 4.13

A time series analysis of sales volumes each quarter for the last three years, 20X6 to 20X8, has identified the trend equation as follows:

$y = 400 + 105x$

where y is the sales volume and x is the time period.

The seasonal variations for each quarter have been calculated as:

Quarter 1	−175
Quarter 2	+225
Quarter 3	+150
Quarter 4	−200

Estimate the actual sales volume for each quarter of 20X9.

Quarter 1		units
Quarter 2		units
Quarter 3		units
Quarter 4		units

Chapter 5

Task 5.1

Write a brief memo to a new accounts assistant explaining what factors should be taken into account when setting the standard cost of labour for a product.

MEMORANDUM

To: New Accounts Assistant

From: Accountant

Date: xx/xx/xx

Subject: **Setting the standard cost of labour**

....

Task 5.2

A business budgeted to produce 2,680 units of one of its products during the month of May. The product uses 5 kg of raw material with a standard cost of £4.00 per kg. During the month the actual production was 2,800 units using 14,400 kg of raw materials costing £60,480.

Calculate the following variances:

	Variance £	Adverse/Favourable
Total materials cost variance		
Materials price variance		
Materials usage variance		

....

Task 5.3

A business has the following standard cost card for one unit of its product:

Direct materials	4 kg @ £3 per kg	£12
Direct labour	3 hours @ £9 per hour	£27
Fixed overheads	3 hours @ £4 per hour	£12

The budgeted production level is 12,000 units.

The actual results for the period are:

Production	11,400 units	
Materials 44,800 kgs	£150,480	

Calculate the following variances:

	Variance £	Adverse/Favourable
Total materials cost variance		
Materials price variance		
Materials usage variance		

Task 5.4

Production of product Z1 for the month of November in a manufacturing business was 12,100 units using 54,900 hours of direct labour costing £410,200. The standard cost card shows that the standard labour input for a unit of Z1 is 4.5 hours at a rate of £7.30 per hour.

Calculate the following variances:

	Variance £	Adverse/Favourable
Total labour cost variance		
Labour rate variance		
Labour efficiency variance		

Task 5.5

Production of product X for the month of January was 10,680 units using 53,600 hours of direct labour costing £531,800. The standard cost card shows that the standard labour input for a unit of X is 5 hours at a rate of £10 per hour.

Calculate the following variances:

	Variance £	Adverse/Favourable
Total labour cost variance		
Labour rate variance		
Labour efficiency variance		

Task 5.6

A business has the following standard cost card for one unit of its product:

Direct materials	4 kg @ £3 per kg	£12
Direct labour	3 hours @ £9 per hour	£27
Fixed overheads	3 hours @ £4 per hour	£12

The budgeted production level is 12,000 units.

The actual results for the period are:

| Production | 11,400 units |
| Labour 34,700 hours | £316,400 |

Calculate the following variances:

	Variance £	Adverse/Favourable
Total labour cost variance		
Labour rate variance		
Labour efficiency variance		

Task 5.7

A business has budgeted to produce and sell 10,000 units of its single product. The standard cost per unit is as follows:

Direct materials	£18
Direct labour	£13
Fixed production overhead	£7

During the period the actual results were:

| Production and sales | 11,500 units |
| Fixed production overheads | £75,000 |

The fixed overhead expenditure variance is £ [   ]

The fixed overhead volume variance is £ [   ]

Task 5.8

A business has a single product into which fixed overheads are absorbed on the basis of labour hours. The standard cost card shows that fixed overheads are to be absorbed on the basis of 6 labour hours per unit at a rate of £7.60 per hour. The budgeted level of production is 50,000 units.

The actual results for the period were that fixed overheads were £2,200,000, the actual hours worked were 310,000 and the actual units produced were 52,000.

Calculate the following variances:

	Variance £	Adverse/Favourable
Fixed overhead expenditure variance		
Fixed overhead volume variance		
Fixed overhead efficiency variance		
Fixed overhead capacity variance		

Task 5.9

A business incurred fixed overheads of £203,000 in the month of May. The fixed overheads are absorbed into units of production at the rate of £3.60 per direct labour hour. The actual production during the month was 13,200 units although the budget had been for 14,000 units. The standard labour cost for the production is 4 hours per unit at an hourly rate of £8.00. During the month 50,000 labour hours were worked at a total cost of £403,600.

Calculate the following figures:

(i) The budgeted fixed overhead for the month was £ ☐

(ii) The fixed overhead expenditure variance was £ ☐

(iii) The fixed overhead volume variance was £ ☐

(iv) The fixed overhead efficiency variance was £ ☐

(v) The fixed overhead capacity variance was £ ☐

Task 5.10

The standard cost card for a business's product is shown below:

	£
Direct materials 4.8 kg at £2.80 per kg	13.44
Direct labour 2.5 hours at £8.50 per hour	21.25
Fixed overheads 2.5 hours at £1.60 per hour	4.00
	38.69

The budgeted production was for 1,100 units in the month of July. The actual costs during the month of July for the production of 1,240 units were as follows:

	£
Direct materials 5,800 kg	17,100
Direct labour 3,280 hours	27,060
Fixed overheads	4,650

The following variances have been calculated:

Materials price	£860 Adv
Materials usage	£426 Fav
Labour rate	£820 Fav
Labour efficiency	£1,530 Adv
Fixed overhead expenditure	£250 Adv
Fixed overhead efficiency	£288 Adv
Fixed overhead capacity	£848 Fav

Calculate the budgeted cost of 1,240 units of production and insert the variances in the correct place in the following operating statement. Total the variances and reconcile the budgeted cost of actual production to the actual cost of actual production.

	Adverse £	Favourable £	Total £
Budgeted cost of actual production			

Variances			
Materials price			
Materials usage			
Labour rate			
Labour efficiency			
Fixed overhead expenditure			
Fixed overhead efficiency			
Fixed overhead capacity			
Total variances			
Actual cost of actual production			

Task 5.11

XYZ Ltd is planning to make 120,000 units per period of a new product. The following standards have been set.

		Per unit
Direct material A		1.2 kgs at £11 per kg
Direct material B		4.7 kgs at £6 per kg
Direct labour:	Operation 1	42 minutes
	Operation 2	37 minutes
	Operation 3	11 minutes

Overheads are absorbed at the rate of £30 per labour hour. All direct operatives are paid at the rate of £8 per hour.

What is the standard cost of one unit?

A £41.40

B £53.40

C £83.40

D £98.40

Task 5.12

A manufacturing company has provided you with the following data which relates to component RYX, for the period which has just ended.

	Budget	Actual
Number of labour hours	8,400	7,980
Production units	1,200	1,100
Overhead cost (all fixed)	£22,260	£25,536

Overheads are absorbed at a rate per standard labour hour.

Which of the following is the overhead capacity variance?

A   £5,131 Adverse

B   £3,276 Adverse

C   £742 Adverse

D   £1,113 Adverse

Task 5.13

Which variances do not exist in a marginal costing system?

A   Fixed overhead efficiency variance and fixed overhead capacity variance

B   Fixed overhead expenditure variance and fixed overhead volume variance

C   Fixed overhead expenditure variance and fixed overhead efficiency variance

D   Fixed overhead expenditure variance and fixed overhead capacity variance.

Task 5.14

You are employed as part of the management accounting team in a large industrial company which operates a four-weekly system of management reporting. Your division makes a single product, the Omega, and, because of the nature of the production process, there is no work in progress at any time.

The group management accountant has completed the calculation of the material and labour standard costing variances for the current period to 1 April but has not had the time to complete any other variances. Details of the variances already calculated are reproduced in the working papers below, along with other standard costing data.

Standard costing and budget data – four weeks ended 1 April			
	Quantity	Unit price	Cost per unit
Material (kgs)	7	£25.00	£175
Labour (hours)	40	£7.50	£300
Fixed overheads (hours)	40	£12.50	£500
			£975
	Units	Standard unit cost	Standard cost of production
Budgeted production for the four weeks	4,100	£975	£3,997,500

Working papers

Actual production and expenditure for the four weeks ended 1 April

Units produced	3,850
Cost of 30,000 kgs of materials consumed	£795,000
Cost of 159,000 labour hours worked	£1,225,000
Expenditure on fixed overheads	£2,195,000

Material and labour variances

Material price variance	£45,000 (A)
Material usage variance	£76,250 (A)
Labour rate variance	£32,500 (A)
Labour efficiency variance	£37,500 (A)

(a) Calculate the following variances.

    (i)   The fixed overhead expenditure variance

    (ii) The fixed overhead volume variance

    (iii) The fixed overhead capacity variance

    (iv) The fixed overhead efficiency variance

(b) The production director, who has only recently been appointed, is unfamiliar with fixed overhead variances. Because of this, the group management accountant has asked you to prepare a report to the production director.

    Your report should do the following.

    (i)   Outline the similarities and differences between fixed overhead variances and other cost variances such as the material and labour variances.

(ii) Explain what is meant by the fixed overhead expenditure, volume, capacity and efficiency variances, and show, by way of examples, how these can be of help to the production director in the planning and controlling of the division.

REPORT

To: Production Director

From: Assistant Management Accountant

Date: xx/xx/xx

Subject: **Fixed overhead variances**

Similarities between fixed overhead variances and other variances

The meaning of fixed overhead variances

Fixed overhead variances and planning and control

··

Task 5.15

Choose from the picklist below to show which account the material usage variance will be included in.

Stores control, work in progress control, production overhead control, wages control.

··

Task 5.16

You are employed as a management accountant in the head office of Travel Holdings plc. Travel Holdings owns a number of transport businesses. One of them is Travel Ferries Ltd. Travel Ferries operates ferries which carry passengers and vehicles across a large river. Each year, standard costs are used to develop the budget for Travel Ferries Ltd. The latest budgeted and actual operating results are reproduced below.

Travel Ferries Ltd				
Budgeted and actual operating results for the year to 30 November 20X8				
Operating data		*Budget*		*Actual*
Number of ferry crossings		6,480		5,760
Operating hours of ferries		7,776		7,488
Cost data		£		£
Fuel	1,244,160 litres	497,664	1,232,800 litres	567,088
Labour	93,312 hours	699,840	89,856 hours	696,384
Fixed overheads		466,560		472,440
Cost of operations		1,664,064		1,735,912

Other accounting information

- Fuel and labour are variable costs.

- Fixed overheads are absorbed on the basis of budgeted operating hours.

One of your duties is to prepare costing information and a standard costing reconciliation statement for the chief executive of Travel Holdings.

(a) Calculate the following information.

(1) The standard price of fuel per litre

(2) The standard litres of fuel for 5,760 ferry crossings

(3) The standard labour rate per hour

(4) The standard labour hours for 5,760 ferry crossings

(5) The standard fixed overhead cost per budgeted operating hour

(6) The standard operating hours for 5,760 crossings

(7) The standard fixed overhead cost absorbed by the actual 5,760 ferry crossings

(b) Using the data provided in the operating results and your answers to part (i), calculate the following variances.

(1) The material price variance for the fuel

(2) The material usage variance for the fuel

(3) The labour rate variance

(4) The labour efficiency variance

(5) The fixed overhead expenditure variance

(6) The fixed overhead volume variance

(7) The fixed overhead capacity variance

(8) The fixed overhead efficiency variance

(c) Prepare a statement reconciling the actual cost of operations to the standard cost of operations for the year to 30 November 20X8.

Statement reconciling the actual cost of operations to the standard cost of operations for year ended 30 November 20X8

Number of ferry crossings		
	£	£
Actual cost of operations		
Cost variances		
Material price for fuel		
Material usage for fuel		
Labour rate		
Labour efficiency		
Fixed overhead expenditure		
Fixed overhead capacity		
Fixed overhead efficiency		
Standard cost of operations		

Chapter 6

Task 6.1

State possible reasons for each of the following variances which are all independent of each other.

Variance	Possible causes
Favourable materials price variance	
Favourable materials usage variance	
Adverse labour rate variance	
Adverse labour efficiency variance	

Task 6.2

What possible effect will the following scenarios have on the variances?

Scenario	Possible effects
A business has had to use a less-skilled grade of labour in its production process	
A factory had a machine breakdown which resulted in three days of production delays last month.	

Task 6.3

Given below is the operating statement for a manufacturing business for the last month:

Reconciliation of standard cost of actual production to actual cost – March 20X9

	Variances		
	Adverse	Favourable	
	£	£	£
Standard cost of actual production			672,500
Variances:			
Materials price	24,300		
Materials usage		6,780	
Labour rate	10,600		
Labour efficiency		10,300	
Fixed overhead expenditure		7,490	
Fixed overhead capacity		4,800	
Fixed overhead efficiency		6,100	
	34,900	35,470	
Add: adverse variances			34,900
Less: favourable variances			(35,470)
Actual cost of production			671,930

A number of factors about the month's production have been discovered:

- At the end of the previous month a new warehouse had been purchased which has meant a saving in warehouse rental

- Six new machines were installed at the start of the month which are more power efficient than the old machines, but also more expensive, causing a larger depreciation charge

- There was an unexpected increase in the materials price during the month and when other suppliers were contacted it was found that they were all charging approximately the same price for the materials

- A higher than normal skilled grade of labour was used during the month due to staff shortages. The production process is a skilled process and the benefit has been that these employees, although more expensive, have produced the goods faster and with less wastage. This particular group of employees are also keen to work overtime and, as the business wishes to build up inventory (stock) levels, advantage of this has been taken.

Suggest what effect the combination of the factors given above might have had on the reported variances and make suggestions as to any action that should be taken in light of these factors.

....

Task 6.4

The standard direct materials cost for a business's product is:

6 kg @ £8.00 per kg = £48.00

During the month of October production was 7,400 units of the product and the actual materials cost was £397,400 for 45,100 kgs. The price of the materials has been unexpectedly increased to £8.50 per kg for the whole month.

The total materials price variance is £ [   ]

The planning element of the materials price variance that has been caused by the price increase is £ [   ]

The control element of the materials price variance caused by other factors is £ [   ]

Task 6.5

A business's product has a standard direct material cost of £26.00 (4 kgs @ £6.50 per kg). During the month of March the total production of the product was 2,500 units using 10,600 kgs of materials at a total cost of £73,140. During the month the price was unexpectedly increased due to a shortage of the material to £7.00 per kg.

The total materials price variance is £ [   ]

The planning variance due to price increase is £ [   ]

The control variance due to other factors is £ [   ]

Task 6.6

A business makes a product which uses a raw material which has a standard cost of £7.00 per kg. Each unit of the product requires 5 kgs of this material. The price of the materials for the last few years has been subjected to a time series analysis and the following seasonal variations have been seen to occur.

Jan–Mar	–£0.42
Apr–June	+£0.56
July–Aug	+£0.77
Sept–Dec	–£0.91

During March 18,000 units of the product were made and the price paid for the 92,000 kgs of material was £631,200.

The total materials price variance is £ [   ]

The planning variance due to the season is £ [   ]

The control variance due to other factors is £ [   ]

Task 6.7

The standard cost of direct materials for a product is made up of 8 kgs of material at an average standard cost of £4.00 per kg. It has been noted over the years that the cost of the material fluctuates on a seasonal basis around the average standard cost as follows:

Jan–Mar	+£0.48
Apr–June	+£0.72
July–Sept	–£0.64
Oct–Dec	–£0.56

In the month of June the actual production was 5,000 units and 42,300 kgs of material were used at a cost of £194,580.

The total materials price variance is £ [ ]

The planning variance caused by the seasonal price change is £ [ ]

The control variance caused by other factors is £ [ ]

....

Task 6.8

A business sets the standard cost of its materials at 5kg per unit at a price of £20 per kg, when the index for this particular materials price was 120. During January, 9,000 units were produced using 46,000 kg of material at a total cost of £946,000. In January, the index of the materials price stood at 130.

The total materials price variance is £ [ ]

The planning variance caused by the index change is £ [ ]

The control variance caused by other factors is £ [ ]

....

Task 6.9

You are employed as the assistant management accountant in the group accountant's office of Hampstead plc. Hampstead recently acquired Finchley Ltd, a small company making a specialist product called the Alpha. Standard marginal costing is used by all the companies within the group and, from 1 August 20X8, Finchley Ltd will also be required to use standard marginal costing in its management reports. Part of your job is to manage the implementation of standard marginal costing at Finchley Ltd.

John Wade, the managing director of Finchley, is not clear how the change will help him as a manager. He has always found Finchley's existing absorption costing system sufficient. By way of example, he shows you a summary of his management accounts for the three months to 31 May 20X8. These are reproduced below.

Statement of budgeted and actual cost of Alpha production – 3 months ended 31 May 20X8					
	Actual		**Budget**		**Variance**
Alpha production (units)	10,000		12,000		
	Inputs	£	*Inputs*	£	£
Materials	32,000 m	377,600	36,000 m	432,000	54,400
Labour	70,000 hrs	422,800	72,000 hrs	450,000	27,200
Fixed overhead absorbed		330,000		396,000	66,000
Fixed overhead unabsorbed		75,000		0	(75,000)
		1,205,400		1,278,000	72,600

John Wade is not convinced that standard marginal costing will help him to manage Finchley. 'My current system tells me all I need to know,' he said. 'As you can see, we are £72,600 below budget which is really excellent given that we lost production as a result of a serious machine breakdown.'

To help John Wade understand the benefits of standard marginal costing, you agree to prepare a statement for the three months ended 31 May 20X8 reconciling the standard cost of production to the actual cost of production.

(a) Write a short memo to John Wade:

Your memo should:

(i) Use the budget data to determine the following.

(1) The standard marginal cost per Alpha

(2) The standard cost of actual Alpha production for the three months to 31 May 20X8

(ii) Calculate the following variances.

(1) Material price variance
(2) Material usage variance
(3) Labour rate variance
(4) Labour efficiency variance
(5) Fixed overhead expenditure variance

(iii) include a statement reconciling the actual cost of production to the standard cost of production;

(iv) give TWO reasons why your variances might differ from those in his original management accounting statement, despite using the same basic data;

(v) **briefly** discuss ONE further reason why your reconciliation statement provides improved management information.

MEMO

To: Managing Director

From: Assistant Management Accountant

Date: xx/xx/xx

Subject: The use of standard marginal costing at Finchley Ltd

(i)   (1)   **Standard marginal cost of a unit of Alpha**
      (2)   **Standard cost of producing 10,000 units of Alpha**

(ii) Variance calculations

    (1)   Material price variance
    (2)   Material usage variance
    (3)   Labour rate variance
    (4)   Labour efficiency variance
    (5)   Fixed overhead expenditure variance

(iii)

Reconciliation statement			£
Standard cost of output			
Variances	*Adv*	*Fav*	
	£	£	
Materials price			
Materials usage			
Labour rate			
Labour efficiency			
Fixed overhead expenditure			
Actual cost of output			

(iv) **Reasons for differences**

(v)   **Improved management information**

(b)   On receiving your memo, John Wade informs you that the machine breakdown resulted in the workforce having to be paid for 12,000 hours even though no production took place, and that an index of material prices stood at 466.70 when the budget was prepared but at 420.03 when the material was purchased.

Using this new information, prepare a revised statement reconciling the standard cost of production to the actual cost of production. Your statement should subdivide both the labour variances into those parts arising from the machine breakdown and those parts arising from normal production, and the material price variance into that part due to the change in the index and that part arising for other reasons.

....

Task 6.10

(a) You are the assistant management accountant at the Bare Foot Hotel complex on the tropical island of St Nicolas. The hotel complex is a luxury development. All meals and entertainment are included in the price of the holiday and guests only have to pay for drinks.

The Bare Foot Hotel complex aims to create a relaxing atmosphere. Because of this, meals are available throughout the day and guests can eat as many times as they wish.

The draft performance report for the hotel for the seven days ended 27 November 20X8 is reproduced below.

	Notes	Budget		Actual
Bare Foot Hotel Complex				
Draft performance report for seven days ended 27 November 20X8				
Guests		540		648
		£	£	£	£
Variable costs				
Meal costs	1		34,020		49,896
Catering staff costs	2,3		3,780		5,280
Total variable costs			37,800		55,176
Fixed overhead costs				
Salaries of other staff		5,840		6,000	
Local taxes		4,500		4,200	
Light, heat and power		2,500		2,600	
Depreciation of buildings and equipment		5,000		4,000	
Entertainment		20,500		21,000	
Total fixed overheads			38,340		37,800
Total cost of providing for guests			76,140		92,976

Notes

1   Budgeted cost of meals: number of guests × 3 meals per day × 7 days × £3 per meal

2   Budgeted cost of catering staff: each member of the catering staff is to prepare and serve 12 meals per hour. Cost = (number of guests × 3 meals per day × 7 days ÷ 12 meals per hour) × £4 per hour.

3   Actual hours worked by catering staff = 1,200 hours

Other notes

The amount of food per meal has been kept under strict portion control. Since preparing the draft performance report, however, it has been discovered that guests have eaten, on average, four meals per day.

You report to Alice Groves, the general manager of the hotel, who feels that the format of the draft performance report could be improved to provide her with more meaningful management information. She suggests that the budgeted and actual data given in the existing draft performance report is rearranged in the form of a standard costing report, using absorption costing.

(i)   Use the budget data, the actual data and the notes to the performance report to calculate the following for the seven days ended 27 November 20X8.

   (1)   The actual number of meals served

   (2)   The standard number of meals which should have been served for the actual number of guests

   (3)   The actual hourly rate paid to catering staff

   (4)   The standard hours allowed for catering staff to serve three meals per day for the actual number of guests

   (5)   The standard fixed overhead per guest

   (6)   The total standard cost for the actual number of guests

(ii)   Use the data given in the task and your answers to part (a) (i) to calculate the following variances for the seven days ended 27 November 20X8.

   (1)   The material price variance for meals served

   (2)   The material usage variance for meals served

   (3)   The labour rate variance for catering staff

   (4)   The labour efficiency variance for catering staff, based on a standard of three meals served per guest per day

   (5)   The fixed overhead expenditure variance

   (6)   The fixed overhead volume variance on the assumption that the fixed overhead absorption rate is based on the budgeted number of guests per seven days

(iii)   Prepare a statement reconciling the standard cost for the actual number of guests to the actual cost for the actual number of guests for the seven days ended 27 November 20X8.

(b) On receiving your reconciliation statement, Alice Groves asks the following questions.

– How much of the labour efficiency variance is due to guests taking, on average, four meals per day rather than the three provided for in the budget and how much is due to other reasons?

– Would it be feasible to subdivide the fixed overhead volume variance into a capacity and efficiency variance?

Write a memo to Alice Groves. Your memo should do the following.

(i) Divide the labour efficiency variance into that part due to guests taking more meals than planned and that part due to other efficiency reasons.

(ii) Explain the meaning of the fixed overhead capacity and efficiency variances.

(iii) Briefly discuss whether or not it is feasible to calculate the fixed overhead capacity and efficiency variances for the Bare Foot Hotel complex.

MEMO

To: Alice Groves, general manager

From: Assistant management accountant

Date: xx.xx.xx

Subject: **Performance report** for seven days ended 27 November 20X8

(i) **Subdivision of the catering labour efficiency variance**

(ii) **The meaning of the fixed overhead capacity and efficiency variances**

(iii) **Calculating the fixed overhead capacity and efficiency variances for the Bare Foot Hotel complex**

Chapter 7

Task 7.1

Given below are the production figures for a factory for the last four months.

	November	December	January	February
Output in units	64,300	68,900	62,100	60,200
Budgeted output	65,000	65,000	60,000	62,000
Hours worked	98,200	107,300	90,200	92,000

The standard time for each unit of production is 1.5 hours.

Complete the table to calculate the following performance indicators for each of the four months:

	November	December	January	February
Actual hours per unit				
Efficiency ratio				
Capacity ratio				
Activity ratio				

Task 7.2

Suggest possible measures of productivity for each of the following types of organisation:

Organisation	Possible productivity measures
Taxi firm	
Hospital	
Motorbike courier service	
Firm of accountants	
Retail store	
Maker of hand-made pottery	

Task 7.3

You are given the following information about a small manufacturing business for the year ending 31 March:

Sales revenue	£1,447,600
Cost of materials used	£736,500
Cost of bought in services	£316,900
Number of employees	15

The total value added is £ ☐

The value added per employee is £ ☐

··

Task 7.4

Given below are production and sales figures for a manufacturing organisation for the last three months:

	January	February	March
Production costs	£552,300	£568,500	£629,500
Production wages	£104,800	£98,300	£110,800
Output in units	8,540	8,670	9,320
Hours worked	8,635	7,820	9,280
Budgeted output	8,500	8,200	9,500
Sales revenue	£916,000	£923,000	£965,000
Number of employees	55	55	58

Production costs are made up of the materials for production and the bought in services required in the month. It is estimated that each unit takes 1.1 hours to produce.

(a) Complete the table to calculate the performance indicators for each of the last three months:

	January	February	March
Productivity per labour hour			
Efficiency ratio			
Capacity ratio			
Activity ratio			
Value added per employee			

(b) Comment briefly on what the performance indicators show about the business.

··

Task 7.5

Given below is the summarised production information for a manufacturing organisation for the last month:

Budgeted production in units	15,000
Actual production in units	14,200
Labour hours worked	46,000
Standard hours for each unit	3

(a) Complete the table to calculate the following performance indicators and briefly explain what each one means:

	Calculation	Explanation
Efficiency ratio		
Capacity ratio		
Production volume ratio		

(b) If the workforce had operated at 95% efficiency how many labour hours would have been saved last month?

Task 7.6

Given below is the income statement (profit and loss account) for a business for the year ending 31 March 20X9 and a statement of financial position (balance sheet) at that date.

Income statement

	£	£
Revenue (turnover)		2,650,400
Cost of sales		
Opening inventory (stock)	180,000	
Purchases	1,654,400	
	1,834,400	
Less: closing inventory	191,200	
		1,643,200
Gross profit		1,007,200
Less: expenses		
Selling and distribution costs	328,400	
Administration expenses	342,200	
		670,600
Operating profit		336,600
Interest payable		36,000
Profit after interest		300,600

Statement of financial position

	£	£
Non-current (fixed assets)		1,920,400
Current assets:		
Inventory	191,200	
Receivables (debtors)	399,400	
Bank	16,800	
	607,400	
Payables (creditors)	(190,300)	
Net current assets		417,100
		2,337,500
Less: long term loan		600,000
		1,737,500
Share capital		1,000,000
Other reserves		150,000
Retained earnings (profit and loss reserve)		587,500
		1,737,500

(a) Using the income statement and statement of financial position complete the table to calculate the performance indicators:

Gross profit margin	
Operating profit margin	
Return on capital employed	
Asset turnover	
Non-current asset turnover	
Current ratio	
Quick ratio	
Receivables' collection period	
Inventory turnover period in days	
Payables' payment period	
Interest cover	
Gearing ratio	

(b) If the payables' payment period was increased to 60 days what effect would this have on the cash balance?

Task 7.7

Given below is a summary of a business's performance for the last six months:

	July £'000	Aug £'000	Sept £'000	Oct £'000	Nov £'000	Dec £'000
Sales	560	540	500	550	580	600
Cost of sales	370	356	330	374	400	415
Expenses	123	119	110	116	122	131
Interest payable	–	–	–	3	3	3
Shareholders' funds	440	445	458	468	480	490
Loan	–	–	–	50	50	50

(a) For each month of the year complete the table to calculate the performance indicators:

	July	Aug	Sept	Oct	Nov	Dec
Gross profit margin						
Operating profit margin						
% of expenses to sales						
Return on capital employed						
Asset turnover						

(b) Comment on what the figures calculated in part (a) show about the performance of the business over the last six months.

Task 7.8

Given below is a summary of the performance of a business for the last three years:

	20X6	20X7	20X8
	£'000	£'000	£'000
Sales	1,420	1,560	1,740
Cost of sales	850	950	1,080
Expenses	370	407	469
Interest	–	7	6
Share capital and reserves	1,500	1,600	1,700
Long term loan	–	100	100
Non-current assets	1,100	1,300	1,500
Receivables	155	198	230
Inventory	105	140	190
Payables	140	162	193
Bank balance	280	224	73

(a) For each of the three years complete the table to calculate the performance measures.

(b) Comment on what the measures indicate about the performance of the business over the period:

	20X6	20X7	20X8
Gross profit margin			
Operating profit margin			
Return on capital employed			
Asset turnover			
Non-current asset turnover			
Current ratio			
Quick ratio			
Receivables' collection period			
Inventory turnover in days			
Payables' payment period			

Task 7.9

A manufacturing business has three small divisions, North, South and Central. The figures for the last three months of 20X6 for each division are given below:

	North	South	Central
	£	£	£
Financial details			
Sales	870,000	560,000	640,000
Opening inventory (stock)	34,000	41,000	34,000
Closing inventory	32,000	29,000	38,000
Purchases	590,000	380,000	420,000
Expenses	121,000	106,000	138,000
Share capital and reserves	980,000	690,000	615,000
Payables	103,400	42,600	66,700
Receivables	100,100	107,300	87,600
Non-financial details			
Factory floor area	500 sq m	400 sq m	420 sq m
Factory employees	18	12	15
Hours worked	8,500	5,800	7,000
Units produced	17,000	10,200	12,300

(a) Complete the table to calculate the performance indicators for each division:

	North	South	Central
Gross profit margin			
Operating profit margin			
Return on capital employed			
Asset turnover			
Inventory turnover in months (using average inventory)			
Receivables' collection period in months			
Payables' collection period in months			
Units produced per square metre of floor area			
Units produced per employee			
Units produced per hour			

(b) Use the performance indicators calculated in (a) to compare the performances of the three divisions for the three-month period.

Task 7.10

(i) A business operates on a gross profit margin of 48% and sales for the period were £380,000. The gross profit is £ [   ]

(ii) A business operates on a gross profit margin of 34% and the gross profit made in the period was £425,000.

The sales for the period were £ [   ]

(iii) A business had sales of £85,000 in a month and with a gross profit margin of 40% and an operating profit margin of 11.5%.

The expenses for the month were £ [   ]

(iv) A business has a return on capital employed of 11.6% and made an operating profit for the period of £100,000.

The capital employed is £ [   ]

(v) A business has a net profit percentage of 8% and a return on capital employed of 10%.

The asset turnover of the business is £ [   ]

(vi) A business has opening inventory and closing inventory of £158,000 and £182,000 and made purchases during the year totalling £560,000.

Inventory turned over [   ] times during the year.

(vii) A business has a receivables' collection period of 48 days and the closing receivables figure is £96,000.

The sales for the year are £ [   ]

Task 7.11

Given below are the summarised income statements and statements of financial position of a business for the last two years.

Summarised income statements

	Y/e 31 Dec 20X8	Y/e 31 Dec 20X7
	£'000	£'000
Revenue	602	564
Cost of sales	329	325
Gross profit	273	239
Expenses	163	143
Operating profit	110	96
Interest payable	10	10
Profit before tax	100	86

Summarised statements of financial position

	31 Dec 20X8		31 Dec 20X7	
	£	£	£	£
Non-current assets		709		632
Current assets:				
Inventory	28		32	
Receivables	66		68	
Cash	2		3	
	96		103	
Payables	55		45	
Net current assets		41		58
		750		690
Long term loan		150		150
		600		540
Share capital		300		300
Retained earnings		300		240
		600		540

(a) Complete the table for each of the two years to calculate the performance indicators, based on total capital employed when relevant.

	31 Dec 20X8	31 Dec 20X7
Gross profit margin		
Operating profit margin		
Return on capital employed		
Asset turnover		
Non-current asset turnover		
Current ratio		
Quick ratio		
Receivables' collection period		
Inventory turnover in days		
Payables' payment period		
Interest cover		
Gearing ratio		

(b) Comment upon the performance of the business for the last two years basing your comments on the performance indicators calculated in part (a).

Task 7.12

Middle plc owns two subsidiaries, East Ltd and West Ltd, producing soft drinks. Both companies rent their premises and both use plant of similar size and technology. Middle plc requires the plant in the subsidiaries to be written off over ten years using straight-line depreciation and assuming zero residual values.

East Ltd was established five years ago but West Ltd has only been established for two years. Goods returned by customers generally arise from quality failures and are destroyed. Financial and other data relating to the two companies are reproduced below.

Income statements year to 30 November 20X8			Statements of financial position extracts at 30 November 20X8		
	West Ltd	East Ltd		West Ltd	East Ltd
	£'000	£'000		£'000	£'000
Revenue	18,000	17,600	Plant	16,000	10,000
Less Returns			Depreciation to	3,200	5,000
	90	176	date		
Net revenue	17,910	17,424	Non-current assets	12,800	5,000
Material	2,000	2,640	Current assets	4,860	3,000
Labour	4,000	4,840	Current liabilities	(2,320)	(1,500)
Production overheads*	3,000	3,080	Net assets	15,340	6,500
Gross profit	8,910	6,864			
Marketing	2,342	1,454			
Research & development	1,650	1,010			
Training	950	450			
Administration	900	1,155			
Operating profit	3,068	2,795			

*Includes plant depreciation of £1,600,000 for West Ltd and £1,000,000 for East Ltd

Other data (000's litres)	West Ltd	East Ltd
Gross sales	20,000	22,000
Returns	100	220
Net sales	19,900	21,780
Orders received in year	20,173	22,854

You are employed by Middle plc as a member of a team monitoring the performance of subsidiaries within the group. Middle plc aims to provide its shareholders with the best possible return for their investment and to meet customers' expectations. It does this by comparing the performance of subsidiaries and using the more efficient ones for benchmarking.

Your team leader, Angela Wade, has asked you to prepare a report evaluating the performance of West Ltd and East Ltd. Your report should do the following.

(a) Calculate and explain the meaning of the following financial ratios for each company.

(i) The return on capital employed

(ii) The asset turnover

(iii) The sales (or operating profit) margin

(b) Calculate the percentage of faulty sales as a measure of the level of customer service for each company.

(c) Identify ONE other possible measure of the level of customer service which could be derived from the accounting data.

(d) Identify TWO limitations to your analysis in task (a), using the data in the accounts.

(a) **Angela Wade**

    From: **A Technician**

    Date: **xx.xx.xx**

    Subject: **West Ltd and East Ltd – Performance Report**

    (i)   **Return on capital employed (ROCE)**

    (ii) **Asset turnover**

    (iii) **Sales margin**

(b) **Measure of customer service: faulty sales**

(c) **Further measure of customer service**

(d) **Limitations of financial ratios**

....

Task 7.13

(a) You are employed by Micro Circuits Ltd as a financial analyst reporting to Angela Frear, the Director of Corporate Strategy. One of your responsibilities is to monitor the performance of subsidiaries within the group. Financial and other data relating to subsidiary A is reproduced below.

Subsidiary A						
Income statement year to 30 November 20X8			**Extract from statement of financial position at 30 November 20X8**			
	£'000	£'000		£'000	£'000	£'000
Revenue		4,000		*Land and buildings*	*Plant and machinery*	*Total*
less returns		100	Non-current assets			
Net revenue[1]		3,900	Cost	2,000	2,500	4,500
Material	230		Additions	–	1,800	1,800
Labour	400			2,000	4,300	6,300
Production overheads[2]	300		Accumulated dep'n	160	1,700	1,860
Cost of production	930			1,840	2,600	4,440
Opening finished inventory	50					
Closing finished inventory	(140)		Raw material inventory	15		
Cost of sales		840	Finished goods inventory	140		
Gross profit		3,060		155		
Marketing	500		Receivables	325		
Customer support	400		Cash and bank	40		
Research and development	750		Payables	(85)		
Training	140					
Administration	295	2,085				435
Operating profit		975	Net assets			4,875

Other information

Notes

1. **Analysis of revenue**

	£'000		£'000
Regular customers	3,120	New products	1,560
New customers	780	Existing products	2,340
	3,900		3,900

2. Production overheads include £37,200 of reworked faulty production.

3. Orders received in the year totalled £4,550,000.

(a) Angela Frear asks you to calculate the following performance indicators in preparation for a board meeting.

Performance indicator	Workings	
Return on capital employed		
Asset turnover		
Sales (or operating profit) margin		
Average age of receivables in months		
Average age of finished inventory in months		

(b) One of the issues to be discussed at the board meeting is the usefulness of performance indicators. Angela Frear has recently attended a conference on creating and enhancing value.

Three criticisms were made of financial performance indicators.

– They could give misleading signals.

– They could be manipulated.

– They focus on the short term and do not take account of other key, non-financial performance indicators.

At the conference, Angela was introduced to the idea of the balanced scorecard. The balanced scorecard looks at performance measurement from four perspectives.

The financial perspective

This is concerned with satisfying shareholders. Examples include the return on capital employed and sales margin.

The customer perspective

This asks how customers view the business and is concerned with measures of customer satisfaction. Examples include speed of delivery and customer loyalty.

The internal perspective

This looks at the quality of the company's output in terms of technical excellence and customer needs. Examples would be striving towards total quality management and flexible production as well as unit cost.

The innovation and learning perspective

This is concerned with the continual improvement of existing products and the ability to develop new products as customers' needs change. An example would be the percentage of revenue attributable to new products.

Angela Frear asks you to prepare briefing notes for the board meeting. Using the data from part (a) where necessary, your notes should do the following.

(i) Suggest ONE reason why the return on capital employed calculated in (a) might be misleading.

(ii) Identify ONE way of manipulating the sales (or operating profit) margin.

(iii) Calculate the average delay in fulfilling orders.

(iv) Identify ONE other possible measure of customer satisfaction other than the delay in fulfilling orders.

(v) Calculate TWO indicators which may help to measure performance from an internal perspective.

(vi) Calculate ONE performance indicator which would help to measure the innovation and learning perspective.

Briefing notes on the usefulness of performance indicators

Prepared for Angela Frear

Prepared by Financial Analyst

Dated: xx.xx.xx

(i) **Return on capital employed**

(ii) **Sales (operating profit) margin**

    (iii) **Average delay in fulfilling orders**

    (iv) **Measures of customer satisfaction**

    (v) **Measuring performance from an internal perspective**

    (vi) **Measuring the innovation and learning perspective**

....

Task 7.14

(a) Travel Bus Ltd is owned by Travel Holdings plc. It operates in the town of Camford. Camford is an old town with few parking facilities for motorists. Several years ago, the Town Council built a car park on the edge of the town and awarded Travel Bus the contract to carry motorists and their passengers between the car park and the centre of the town.

Originally, the Council charged motorists £4.00 per day for the use of the car park but, to encourage motorists not to take their cars into the town centre, parking has been free since 1 December 20X7.

The journey between the car park and the town centre is the only service operated by Travel Bus Ltd in Camford. A summary of the results for the first two years of operations, together with the net assets associated with the route and other operating data, is reproduced below.

	20X7 £	20X8 £		20X7 £	20X8 £
INcome statement year ended 30 November			**Extract from statement of financial position at 30 November**		
Revenue	432,000	633,600	Buses	240,000	240,000
			Accumulated		
Fuel	129,600	185,328	depreciation	168,000	180,000
Wages	112,000	142,000	Non-current assets	72,000	60,000
Other variable costs	86,720	84,512	Net current assets	14,400	35,040
Gross profit	103,680	221,760		86,400	95,040
Bus road tax and					
insurance	22,000	24,000			
Depreciation of					
buses	12,000	12,000			
Maintenance of					
buses	32,400	28,512			
Fixed garaging costs	29,840	32,140			
Administration	42,000	49,076			
Operating profit/(loss)	(34,560)	76,032			

Other operating data	20X7	20X8
Fare per passenger journey	£0.80	£1.00
Miles per year	324,000	356,400
Miles per journey	18.0	18.0
Days per year	360	360
Wages per driver	£14,000	£14,200

Throughout the two years, the drivers were paid a basic wage per week, no bonuses were paid and no overtime was incurred.

In two weeks there will be a meeting between officials of the Town Council and the chief executive of Travel Holdings to discuss the performance of Travel Bus for the year to 30 November 20X8. The previous year's performance indicators were as follows.

Gross profit margin	24%
Operating profit margin	–8%
Return on capital employed	–40%
Asset turnover	5 times
Number of passengers in the year	540,000
Total cost per mile	£1.44
Number of journeys per day	50
Maintenance cost per mile	£0.10
Passengers per day	1,500
Passengers per journey	30
Number of drivers	8

In preparation for the meeting, you have been asked to calculate the following performance indicators for the year to 30 November 20X8.

		Performance indictor for year to 30 November 20X8
(i)	Gross profit margin	
(ii)	Operating profit margin	
(iii)	Return on capital employed	
(iv)	Asset turnover	
(v)	Number of passengers in the year	
(vi)	Total cost per mile	
(vii)	Number of journeys per day	
(viii)	Maintenance cost per mile	
(ix)	Passengers per day	
(x)	Passengers per journey	
(xi)	Number of drivers	

(b) On receiving your performance indicators, the chief executive of Travel Holdings raises the following issues with you.

- The drivers are claiming that the improved profitability of Travel Bus reflects their increased productivity.

- The managers believe that the change in performance is due to improved motivation arising from the introduction of performance related pay for managers during the year to 30 November 20X8.

- The officials from the Town Council are concerned that Travel Bus is paying insufficient attention to satisfying passenger needs and safety.

The chief executive asks for your advice.

Write a memo to the chief executive of Travel Holdings plc. Where relevant, you should make use of the data and answers to task a) to do the following.

(i) Briefly discuss whether or not increased productivity always leads to increased profitability.

(ii) Develop ONE possible measure of driver productivity and suggest whether or not the drivers' claim is valid.

(iii) Suggest ONE reason, other than improved motivation, why the profitability of Travel Bus might have improved.

(iv) (1) Suggest ONE existing performance indicator which might measure the satisfaction of passenger needs.

   (2) Suggest ONE other possible performance indicator of passenger needs which cannot be measured from the existing performance data collected by Travel Bus.

(v) (1) Suggest ONE existing performance indicator which might measure the safety aspect of Travel Bus's operations.

 (2) Suggest ONE other possible performance indicator which cannot be measured from the existing performance data collected by Travel Bus.

MEMO

To: Chief executive

From: Management accountant

Date: xx.xx.xx

Subject: **Performance of Travel Bus Ltd for the year to 30 November 20X8**

This memo addresses a number of issues concerning the productivity and profitability of Travel Bus Ltd.

(i)   Productivity and profitability

(ii)   Driver productivity

(iii) Reason for improved profitability

(iv)   Performance indicators to measure the satisfaction of passenger needs

(v)   Monitoring the safety aspect of Travel Bus's operations

Task 7.15

TeesRus Ltd makes and packs tea bags. The company currently has 8 Pickmaster machines, which are coming to the end of their useful life. The company is considering replacing all 8 machines with either new Pickmaster machines or new Pickmaster 2 machines.

Each new Pickmaster machine costs £20,000 and requires 10 operators per day for the 100 days of the harvest. The machine will have a life of 10 years and a depreciation charge of £2,000 per year.

A new Pickmaster 2 machine requires only 1 operator per day for the 100 days. This machine costs £90,000 to purchase and will have a life of 10 years. The depreciation charge will be £9,000 per year.

Other budgeted information for 20X8 is as follows:

- The forecast harvest will last 100 days and produce 2.5 million kilograms of tea.

- The selling price of tea will be 45 pence per kilogram.

- Budgeted revenue is £1,125,000.

- Tea picker costs will be £150,000.

- Tea processor operators currently earn £6 per day.

- The tea pickers and tea processor operators are employed as and when needed on temporary contracts.

- Seed and fertiliser costs will be £75,000.

- Administration costs will be £150,000 if the Pickmaster machines are purchased.

- Administration costs will be £135,000 if the Pickmaster 2 machines are purchased.

- Distribution costs will be £350,000.

- The net assets at the end of the period will be £935,500 plus the budgeted operating profit.

- Disposing of the old machines will incur no profit, loss or any depreciation charge during 20X8.

(a) Prepare TWO budgeted income statements and net asset workings assuming that the business purchases either 8 Pickmaster or 8 Pickmaster 2 machines.

Budgeted income statements

	Pickmaster	Pickmaster 2
	£	£
Revenue		
Cost of sales		
Tea pickers		
Tea processor operators		
Depreciation		
Seed and fertiliser costs		
Total cost of sales		
Gross profit		
Administration costs		
Distribution costs		
Operating profit		

Net assets at year end

	Pickmaster	Pickmaster 2
	£	£
Budgeted net assets		
Operating profit		

(b) Complete the table to calculate the following indicators for each option:

	Pickmaster	Pickmaster 2
Gross profit margin		
Operating profit margin		
Return on net assets		

(c) Prepare a report for the managing director to include the following:

  (i) comments on the indicators calculated in part (b) above

  (ii) two other considerations

  (iii) a recommendation whether to purchase the Pickmaster or Pickmaster 2 machines

REPORT

To: Managing Director

From: Accounting technician

Date: December 20X7

Subject: Purchase of new machinery

Performance indicators

Other considerations

Conclusion

....

Task 7.16

BeThere Airlines is reviewing its catering division and has provided the following information for the previous three months. The division has no administration or distribution costs. All costs are treated as costs of sales. All production has to be used in that day.

Catering Division

Cost report for the three-month period

	September £	October £	November £
Revenue	690,000	697,200	672,000
Cost of production			
Direct materials	185,000	185,100	185,220
Direct labour	274,313	275,975	279,300
Fixed production overheads	82,000	82,000	82,000
Total cost of sales	541,313	543,075	546,520
Profit	148,687	154,125	125,480

Catering Division statement of financial position

	September £	October £	November £
Non-current assets			
Land and buildings	800,000	795,000	790,000
Machinery	480,000	460,000	420,000
Current assets			
Inventory of raw materials	231,000	251,500	307,800
Amounts due from Airlines Division	690,000	697,200	672,000
Current liabilities			
Trade payables	190,000	185,000	185,100
Net current assets	731,000	763,700	794,700
Non-current liabilities	800,000	800,000	800,000
Net assets	1,211,000	1,218,700	1,204,700

	Units	Units	Units
Capacity (meals per month)	125,000	125,000	125,000
Meals ordered by Flights Division	115,000	117,000	112,000
Budgeted meals	115,000	117,000	112,000
Meals produced	115,500	116,200	117,600

(a) Calculate the following performance indicators for each month, expressing each answer to two decimal places:

    (i)   Profit margin

    (ii)   Direct material cost as a percentage of revenue

    (iii) Direct labour cost as a percentage of revenue

    (iv) Return on capital employed (ROCE)

    (v)   Meals produced as a percentage of orders

    (vi) Meals produced as a percentage of capacity

(b) Draft a brief report to the managing director commenting on the performance of the division in November. You should base your report on your calculations above.

REPORT

To:	Managing Director
From:	Accounting Technician
Subject:	Performance of the Catering Division
Date:	7 December 20X6

(c) The operations director is now reviewing various alternatives to determine whether it is possible to reduce monthly costs.

She is considering whether to invest in a new machine which:

- Will mechanise part of the process and reduce the labour cost per meal from the current rate of £2.375 to £1.50

- Could either be purchased for £3 million or rented for £50,000 per month

- Is expected to have a life of 10 years and a scrap value of £900,000.

If the company purchases the machine, the division's net assets as at the end of November will increase by £1 million plus the profit for the period.

If the company rents the machine, the division's net assets will only increase by the profit for the period.

The operations director's performance is measured on ROCE, which she would like to see improved.

(i)   Prepare a forecast income statement and net asset calculation (a full statement of financial position is not required) for both options (renting and purchasing) for one month.

Note: Assume that the number of meals produced and sold will be 120,000 per month at a cost of £6 per meal. The material cost will remain as standard at £2 per meal, and monthly overheads will stay at £82,000 before any additional costs of the new machine. Ignore the time value of money.

(ii) Calculate the profit margin and the ROCE for both options.

(iii) What action would you recommend to the operations director?

Chapter 8

Task 8.1

For each of the following state which type of cost of quality it is (prevention, appraisal, internal failure or external failure):

		Type of cost
(i)	lost contribution on defective products sold as seconds	
(ii)	cost of replacing faulty products	
(iii)	claims from customers relating to defective products	
(iv)	products scrapped due to faulty raw materials	
(v)	training for quality control staff	
(vi)	maintenance of quality control equipment	
(vii)	performance testing of finished goods	
(viii)	costs of customer after sales service department	
(ix)	costs of inspection of raw materials	
(x)	costs of production delays due to re-working defective products discovered in quality inspection	

Task 8.2

A clothing manufacturer has had a number of events occurring recently:

(i) the internal designers have designed a new type of zipper that should last much longer than normal zippers and should reduce returns of products

(ii) one line of jumpers produced over the last few months were produced on a faulty machine and have been returned by all the retailers who purchased them as the seams have come apart. Some of the retailers are considering suing the company for losses caused and it is almost certain that they will never purchase from the manufacturer again

(iii) it has been discovered that the fabric used to make a large quantity of men's suits was flawed and these can now only be sold at a drastically reduced price as seconds.

As a result of this discovery the manufacturer has introduced new inspection controls for raw materials.

Analyse each of these events and determine what effects they are likely to have on the various categories of quality costs – prevention, appraisal, internal failure and external failure – by completing the table.

	Prevention	Appraisal	Internal failure	External failure
(i) Zippers				
(ii) Jumpers				
(iii) Men's suits				

Task 8.3

Give three examples of explicit costs of quality and three examples of implicit costs of quality.

Explicit costs of quality

-
-
-

Implicit costs of quality

-
-
-

Task 8.4

A manufacturing business estimates that 3 out of every 1,000 of its products that is sold is defective in some way. When the goods are returned by customers they are replaced free of charge. It is estimated that 70% of customers who buy a faulty product will return it but that all customers who buy a faulty product will not buy from the business again. Each unit costs £10 to manufacture and is sold at a price of £15.

Due to quality inspections it is also estimated that 4,000 defective units a year are discovered before they are sold and these can then be sold as 'seconds' at a price of £11. The quality inspections cost £35,000 each year.

The unit sales of the product are 10 million each year.

Analyse and calculate the explicit costs of quality.

Prevention costs	
Appraisal costs	
Internal failure costs	
External failure costs	

Task 8.5

A manufacturing organisation carries out quality inspections on its product and in the last year 5,200 defective units were discovered and had to be sold as seconds at a price of £108 compared with the normal selling price of £200. The costs of the quality inspections totalled £340,000 for the year.

Sales of the product are 1 million units each year and it is estimated that a further 1 in every 2,000 sales will be defective. Of these it is expected that 60% will be returned by customers and will be replaced free of charge. The cost of producing a unit of the product is £120. The customers who do not return their products are unlikely to buy the company's products again; the company expects satisfied customers to make a repeat purchase annually.

List all of the costs of quality incurred by the business and the amount of that cost if possible. State which type of cost of quality each cost is and whether it is an explicit cost or an implicit cost.

....

Task 8.6

What is life cycle costing?

....

Task 8.7

Barnet Ltd is a small company owned by Hampstead plc. Barnet operates a job costing system making a specialist, expensive piece of hospital equipment.

Existing system

Currently, employees are assigned to individual jobs and materials are requisitioned from stores as needed. The standard and actual costs of labour and materials are recorded for each job. These job costs are totalled to produce the marginal cost of production. Fixed production costs – including the cost of storekeeping and inspection of deliveries and finished equipment – are then added to determine the standard and actual cost of production. Any costs of remedial work are included in the materials and labour for each job.

Proposed system

Carol Johnson, the chief executive of Barnet, has recently been to a seminar on modern manufacturing techniques. As a result, she is considering introducing a Total Quality Management. Barnet would offer suppliers a long-term contract at a fixed price but suppliers would have to guarantee the quality of their materials. This would enable Barnet to reduce the levels of materials inventories held.

In addition, she proposes that the workforce is organised as a single team with flexible work practices. This would mean employees helping each other as necessary, with no employee being allocated a particular job. If a job was delayed, the workforce would work overtime without payment in order for the job to be completed on time. In exchange, employees would be guaranteed a fixed weekly wage and time off when production was slack to make up for any overtime incurred.

Cost of quality

Carol has asked to meet you to discuss the implications of her proposals on the existing accounting system. She is particularly concerned to monitor the **cost of quality**. This is defined as the total of all costs incurred in preventing defects plus those costs involved in remedying defects once they have occurred. It is a single figure measuring all the explicit costs of quality – that is, those costs collected within the accounting system.

Task

In preparation for the meeting, produce **brief** notes. Your notes should:

(a) identify FOUR general headings (or classifications) which make up the **cost of quality**;

(b) give ONE example of a type of cost likely to be found within each category;

(c) assuming Carol Johnson's proposals are accepted, state, with reasons, whether or not:

  (i) a standard costing system would still be of help to the managers;

  (ii) it would still be meaningful to collect costs by each individual job;

(d) identify ONE cost saving in Carol Johnson's proposals which would not be recorded in the existing costing system.

....

Task 8.8

(a) You are employed as the assistant management accountant with Local Engineering Ltd, a company which designs and makes a single product, the X4, used in the telecommunications industry. The company has a goods received store which employs staff who carry out random checks to ensure materials are of the correct specification. In addition to the random checks, a standard allowance is made for failures due to faulty materials at the completion stage and the normal practice is to charge the cost of any remedial work required to the cost of production for the month. Once delivered to the customer, any faults discovered in the X4 during its warranty period become an expense of the customer support department.

At the end of each month, management reports are prepared for the Board of Directors. These identify the cost of running the stores and the number of issues, the cost of production and the number of units manufactured, and the cost of customer support.

Jane Greenwood, Local Engineering's management accountant, has just returned from a board meeting to discuss a letter the company recently received from Universal Telecom, Local Engineering's largest customer. In the letter, Universal Telecom explained that it was determined to maintain its position as a world-class provider of telecommunication services and that there was serious concern about the quality of the units delivered by your company. At the meeting, Local Engineering Ltd's board responded by agreeing to establish a company-wide policy of implementing a Total Quality Management (TQM) programme, commencing with a revised model of the X4. Design work on the new model is scheduled to commence in six month's time.

One aspect of this will involve the management accounting department collecting the cost of quality. This is defined as the total of all costs incurred in preventing defects plus those costs involved in remedying defects once they have occurred within the accounting system – attributable to producing output that is not within its specification.

As a first step towards the implementation of TQM, a meeting of the senior staff in the management accounting department has been called to discuss the role the department can play in making TQM a success. Jane Greenwood has asked you to prepare a brief background paper for the meeting, using the template provided.

Your paper should do the following.

(i)   Explain in outline what is meant by Total Quality Management.

(ii) Briefly discuss why the current accounting system fails to highlight the cost of quality.

(iii) Identify FOUR general categories (or classifications) of Local Engineering's activities where expenditure making up the explicit cost of quality will be found.

(iv) Give ONE example of a cost found within each category.

(v)   Give ONE example of a cost of quality not normally identified by the accounting system.

Background paper for meeting

To: Jane Greenwood, Management Accountant

From: Assistant Management Accountant

Subject: Total quality management and the cost of quality

Date: xx/xx/xx

(i)   **The meaning of Total Quality Management**

(ii) **Failure of the current accounting system to highlight the cost of quality**

(iii)/(iv) **Explicit costs of quality**

(v) **Quality costs not identified by the accounting system**

(b) Local Engineering Ltd has capacity to produce no more than 1,000 X4s per month and currently is able to sell all production immediately at a unit selling price of £1,250. A major component of the X4 is a complex circuit board. Spot checks are made on these boards by a team of specialist employees when they are received into stores. In May, 100 units were found to be faulty and returned to the supplier. Good components are then issued to production along with other material.

Upon completion, each X4 is tested. If there is a fault, this involves further remedial work prior to dispatch to customers. For the month of May, 45 units of the X4 had to be reworked because of subsequent faults discovered in the circuit board. This remedial work cost an additional £13,500 in labour charges.

Should a fault occur after delivery to the customer, Local Engineering is able to call upon a team of self-employed engineers to rectify the fault as part of its customer support function. The cost of the remedial work by the self-employed engineers carried out in May – and the number of times they were used – is shown as contractors under customer support.

Extract from the accounting records of Local Engineering Ltd for the month of May

	Units	£		Units	£
Purchases:			**Production:**		
Printed circuits	1,000	120,000	Printed circuits	900	108,000
Less returns	(100)	(12,000)	Other material		121,500
Net costs	900	108,000	Labour		193,500
Other material		121,500	Direct prod'n o/hd		450,000
Total purchases issued to production		229,500	Cost of production		873,000
Other direct stores costs:					
Goods received, labour costs and rent		54,000	**Customer support:**		
Inspection costs		10,000			
Costs of returns	100	4,500	Contractors	54	24,300
Costs of stores		68,500			24,300

As part of the continuing development of Total Quality Management, you are asked by Jane Greenwood to calculate the following:

(i)   The explicit **cost of quality** for Local Engineering Ltd for the month of May

(ii) A further **cost of quality** not reported in the above accounting records.

Task 8.9

(a) Explain the five stages of the product life cycle and how costs and income will alter in each of the five stages.

(b) How does knowledge of the product life cycle affect forecasting of future sales?

Task 8.10

A company is developing a new product. There are currently several other companies manufacturing similar products which sell for a price of £50 each. The company wishes to make a margin of 20%.

The target cost of the new product is £ [   ]

Task 8.11

A company can sell 10,000 units in the next year, giving total sales of £250.000. The company wants to make a profit margin of 70%.

The target cost per unit is £ [   ]

Answer bank

Chapter 1

Task 1.1

True ☐

False ☑

	16,000 units	22,000 units
Total cost	£54,400	£68,200
Cost per unit	£3.40	£3.10

Therefore this is not a variable cost – if it were a true variable cost then the cost per unit would be the same at each activity level.

Task 1.2

Cost	Behaviour
Cost I	Variable
Cost II	Semi-variable or stepped
Cost III	Fixed
Cost IV	Variable

Task 1.3

Activity level – units	Total production cost – £	Cost per unit – £
8,000	50,600	6.325
12,000	63,400	5.283
15,000	73,000	4.867

Workings

	8,000 units £	12,000 units £	15,000 units £
Variable costs			
£32,000/10,000 x 8,000	25,600		
£32,000/10,000 x 12,000		38,400	
£32,000/10,000 x 15,000			48,000
Fixed costs	25,000	25,000	25,000
	50,600	63,400	73,000
Cost per unit	£6.325	£5.283	£4.867

....

Task 1.4

Activity level – units	Total supervisors cost £	Supervisors cost per unit – £
500	20,000	40
1,000	40,000	40
1,500	40,000	26.67

Workings

	500 units £	1,000 units £	1,500 units £
Number of supervisors required			
500/750 = 0.67, round up to 1 @ £20,000	20,000		
1,000/750 = 1.33, round up to 2 @ £20,000		40,000	
1,500/750 = 2 @ £20,000			40,000
Cost per unit	£40	£40	£26.67

....

Task 1.5

		Cost behaviour
(i)	Maintenance department costs which are made up of £25,000 of salaries and an average of £500 cost per call out	Semi-variable
(ii)	Machinery depreciation based upon machine hours used	Variable
(iii)	Salary costs of nursery school teachers where one teacher is required for every six children in the nursery	Stepped
(iv)	Rent for a building that houses the factory, stores and maintenance departments	Fixed

Task 1.6

(i)

Production level – units	Total cost of production £	Cost per unit £
1,000	82,000	82.00
1,500	112,500	75.00
2,000	143,000	71.50

Workings

	1,000 units £	1,500 units £	2,000 units £
Direct materials 6kgs × £4.80 × units	28,800	43,200	57,600
Direct labour 4 hours × £7.00 × units	28,000	42,000	56,000
Building costs – fixed	18,000	18,000	18,000
Leased machines	1,200	1,800	2,400
Stores costs £3,000 + £3.00 × units	6,000	7,500	9,000
	82,000	112,500	143,000
Cost per unit	£82.00	£75.00	£71.50

(ii) The cost per unit is decreasing as production quantities increase. This is due to the fact that not all of the costs are variable. The buildings costs are fixed and part of the stores costs are also fixed. For these elements of total cost, as the production quantity increases so the cost per unit decreases. This in turn reduces the total overall unit cost as the quantity increases.

Task 1.7

The variable cost per machine hour is £15.00

The fixed costs of the maintenance department are £72,000

Workings

Variable costs

	Machine hours	Cost £
June (lowest)	14,200	285,000
August (highest)	15,200	300,000
Increase	1,000	15,000
Variable cost = £15,000/1,000 hours		
= £15 per hour		
Fixed costs:		£
June		
Variable element £15 x 14,200 hours		213,000
Fixed element (bal fig)		72,000
Total cost		285,000

....

Task 1.8

(a)   The fixed element of the production cost is £167,000

The variable element of the production cost per unit is £7

Workings

	Activity level	Cost
		£
July (lowest)	63,000	608,000
September (highest)	76,000	699,000
Increase	13,000	91,000
Variable element = £91,000/13,000		
= £7 per unit		
Fixed costs:	£	
July		
Variable element £7 x 63,000 units	441,000	
Fixed element (bal fig)	167,000	
Total cost	608,000	

(b)

Level of production – units	Production cost £
74,000	685,000
90,000	797,000

Workings

(i) Production level of 74,000 units:

	£
Variable cost £7 x 74,000	518,000
Fixed cost	167,000
Total cost	685,000

(ii) Production level of 90,000 units:

	£
Variable cost £7 x 90,000	630,000
Fixed cost	167,000
Total cost	797,000

(c) The estimate for the 74,000 units of production is likely to be more accurate than the estimate for 90,000 units. Estimating the costs at 74,000 units is an example of interpolation, in that the estimate is being made for a production level that is within the range of production levels used to estimate the variable and fixed costs. 90,000 units of production is significantly higher than the levels of production used in estimating fixed and variable costs and therefore it is possible that the costs would behave differently at this level of production. This is an example of extrapolation.

Chapter 2

Task 2.1

Absorption rate method	Cutting rate £	Finishing rate £	Most appropriate 1, 2 or 3
Rate per unit	5.86	4.24	2 - most appropriate where all products are of similar size and require a similar input in terms of time and resources of the departments
Rate per direct labour hour	14.65	1.77	3 - most appropriate in labour intensive departments where most of the overhead relates to labour
Rate per machine hour	4.88	21.20	1 - most appropriate in a largely mechanised department where most of the overhead relates to machinery costs

Workings

		Cutting	Finishing
(a)	Rate per unit	$\frac{58,600}{10,000}$	$\frac{42,400}{10,000}$
		= £5.86 per unit	= £4.24 per unit
(b)	Rate per direct labour hour	$\frac{58,600}{4,000}$	$\frac{42,400}{24,000}$
		= £14.65 per labour hour	= £1.77 per labour hour
(c)	Rate per machine hour	$\frac{58,600}{12,000}$	$\frac{42,400}{2,000}$
		= £4.88 per machine hour	£21.20 per machine hour

Task 2.2

(a)

Department	Overhead absorption rate £
C	£1.25 per machine hour
D	£2.25 per direct labour hour

Workings

$$C = \frac{£125,000}{100,000}$$

= £1.25 per machine hour

as C is a highly mechanised department most of the overhead will relate to the machinery therefore machine hours have been used to absorb the overhead.

$$D = \frac{£180,000}{80,000}$$

= £2.25 per direct labour hour

as D is a highly labour intensive department then most of the overhead will relate to the hours that are worked by the labour force therefore labour hours are used to absorb the overhead.

(b) The overhead to be included in the cost of product P is £22.00

Working

Product P – department C overhead	£1.25 × 5	= £ 6.25
department D overhead	£2.25 × 7	= £15.75
		£22.00

Task 2.3

	Under-absorption £	Over-absorption £	Debit/Credit
Budgeted production was 1,200 units and budgeted overheads were £5,400. Overheads are to be absorbed on a unit basis. The actual production was 1,000 units and the overheads incurred were £5,000.	500		Debit
Budgeted production was 600 units to be produced in 1,800 labour hours. Budgeted overheads of £5,040 are to be absorbed on a direct labour hour basis. The actual production for the period was 700 units in 2,200 labour hours and the actual overheads were £5,100.		1,060	Credit
Budgeted production was 40,000 units and the budgeted machine hours were 2 hours per unit. Budgeted overheads were £320,000 and were to be absorbed on a machine hour basis. The actual overheads incurred were £320,000 and the production was 42,000 units. The total machine hours were 82,000.		8,000	Credit

Workings

(a)	Overhead absorption rate	=	$\dfrac{£5,400}{1,200}$
		=	£4.50 per unit
	Overhead incurred	=	£5,000
	Overhead absorbed		
	1,000 units × £4.50	=	£4,500
	Under-absorbed overhead	=	£500 – a further expense in the income statement (P & L)
(b)	Overhead absorption rate	=	$\dfrac{£5,040}{1,800}$
		=	£2.80 per direct labour hour
	Overhead incurred	=	£5,100
	Overhead absorbed		
	2,200 hours × £2.80	=	£6,160
	Over-absorbed overhead	=	£1,060 – a credit to the income statement

(c) Overhead absorption rate $=$ $\dfrac{£320,000}{80,000}$

$=$ £4.00 per machine hour

Overhead incurred $=$ £320,000

Overhead absorbed

82,000 × £4.00 $=$ £328,000

Over-absorbed overhead $=$ £8,000 – a credit to the income statement

....

Task 2.4

The unit cost under absorption costing will be £39.50

The unit cost under marginal costing will be £37.50

Workings

(a) **Absorption costing**

	£
Direct materials	12.00
Direct labour – Cutting (2 × £7.40)	14.80
Finishing	6.80
Variable overheads:	
Cutting (2 x £1.40)	2.80
Finishing (1 x £1.10)	1.10
Fixed overheads:	
Cutting (2 x £0.60)	1.20
Finishing (1 x £0.80)	0.80
	39.50

(b) **Marginal costing**

	£
Direct materials	12.00
Direct labour – Cutting (2 × £7.40)	14.80
Finishing	6.80
Variable overheads:	
Cutting (2 x £1.40)	2.80
Finishing (1 x £1.10)	1.10
	37.50

Workings: Hourly absorption rates

	Rate per hour
	£
Variable overheads:	
Cutting (£336,000/240,000)	1.40
Finishing (£132,000/120,000)	1.10
Fixed overheads:	
Cutting (£144,000/240,000)	0.60
Finishing (£96,000/120,000)	0.80

Task 2.5

(a) The absorption costing profit for July was £52,800

The absorption costing profit for August was £60,000.

The marginal costing profit for July was £49.100

The marginal costing profit for August was £61,850

Workings

Cost per unit – absorption costing

	£
Direct materials	6.80
Direct labour	3.60
Variable costs (£32,400/24,000)	1.35
Fixed costs (£44,400/24,000)	1.85
	13.60

Cost per unit – marginal costing

	£
Direct materials	6.80
Direct labour	3.60
Variable costs (£32,400/24,000)	1.35
	11.75

Absorption costing – income statement (profit and loss account)

		July		August	
		£	£	£	£
Sales	(22,000 × £16)		352,000		
	(25,000 × £16)				400,000
Less: cost of sales					
Opening inventory (stock)					
	(1,500 × £13.60)	20,400			
	(3,500 × £13.60)			47,600	
Production	(24,000 × £13.60)	326,400		326,400	
		346,800		374,000	
Less: closing inventory					
	(3,500 × £13.60)	(47,600)			
	(2,500 × £13.60)			(34,000)	
			299,200		340,000
Profit			52,800		60,000

Marginal costing – income statement

		July		August	
		£	£	£	£
Sales	(22,000 × £16)		352,000		
	(25,000 × £16)				400,000
Less: cost of sales					
Opening inventory					
	(1,500 × £11.75)	17,625			
	(3,500 × £11.75)			41,125	
Production	(24,000 × £11.75)	282,000		282,000	
		299,625		323,125	
Less: closing inventory					
	(3,500 × £11.75)	(41,125)			
	(2,500 × £11.75)			(29,375)	
			258,500		293,750
Contribution			93,500		106,250
Fixed costs			(44,400)		(44,400)
			49,100		61,850

(b)   Reconciliation of profit figures

	July	*August*
	£	£
Absorption cost profit	52,800	60,000
Increase in inventory (3,500 – 1,500)		
× fixed c.p.u. 2,000 × £1.85	(3,700)	
Decrease in inventory (3,500 – 2,500)		
× fixed c.p.u. 1,000 × £1.85		1,850
Marginal cost profit	49,100	61,850

Task 2.6

(a)   The profit for the quarter under absorption costing is £47,560

The profit for the quarter under marginal costing £48,840

Workings

Unit cost – absorption costing

	£
Direct materials	23.60
Direct labour (4 × £5.80)	23.20
Variable overheads (£88,000/8,000)	11.00
Fixed overheads (£51,200/8,000)	6.40
	64.20

Unit cost – marginal costing

	£
Direct materials	23.60
Direct labour (4 × £5.80)	23.20
Variable overheads (£88,000/8,000)	11.00
	57.80

Absorption costing – income statement (profit and loss account)

	£	£
Sales (8,200 × £70)		574,000
Less: cost of sales		
Opening inventory (stock) (840 × £64.20)	53,928	
Production cost (8,000 × £64.20)	513,600	
	567,528	
Less: closing inventory (640 × £64.20)	(41,088)	
		526,440
Profit		47,560

Marginal costing – income statement

	£	£
Sales (8,200 × £70)		574,000
Less: cost of sales		
Opening inventory (840 × £57.80)	48,552	
Production cost (8,000 × £57.80)	462,400	
	510,952	
Less: closing inventory (640 × £57.80)	(36,992)	
		473,960
Contribution		100,040
Less: fixed costs		(51,200)
Profit		48,840

(b)

	£
Absorption costing profit	47,560
Decrease in inventory × fixed cost per unit (200 × £6.40)	1,280
Marginal costing profit	48,840

Task 2.7

(a) The price of job HMG/012 based upon direct costs plus 50% mark-up is £457,500
The price of job CFG/013 based upon direct costs plus 50% mark-up is £279,000

	HMG/012 £	CFG/013 £
Equipment cost	175,000	120,000
Direct labour cost	130,000	66,000
Total direct cost	305,000	186,000
Mark up	50%	50%
Price	£457,500	£279,000

(b) **Calculation of cost per unit of cost driver**

Activity	Budgeted cost pool	Cost driver	Cost driver units pa	Cost per unit of cost driver
	£			£
Design department	675,000	Design hours	25,000	27.00
Site engineers	370,000	Miles travelled	185,000	2.00
Purchasing department	105,000	Items purchased	15,000	7.00
Payroll department	75,000	Direct hours	300,000	0.25
Site management	750,000	Direct hours	300,000	2.50
Post-installation inspection	80,000	Items purchased	20,000	4.00

Cost pool	Working	Total Cost HMG/012	Total Cost CFG/013
		£	£
Design department	£27 x 1,280/620	34,560	16,740
Site engineers	£2 x (320 x 30)/(90 x 10)	19,200	1,800
Purchasing department	£7 x 650/410	4,550	2,870
Payroll department	£0.25 x 10,000/6,000	2,500	1,500
Site management	£2.50 x 10,000/6,000	25,000	15,000
Post-installation inspection	£4 x 650/410	2,600	1,640
Total cost		88,140	39,550

Task 2.8

	Server allocated overheads £	PC allocated overheads £
Set-up costs	10,000	–
Rent and power (production area)	24,000	96,000
Rent (stores area)	25,000	35,000
Salaries of stores issue staff	8,000	22,000
Total overheads	67,000	153,000

Workings

Reallocation of Little Ltd's budgeted total fixed annual overheads between server and PC production

Step 1. Calculation of cost per cost driver

	Budgeted total annual overheads	Cost driver	Number of cost drivers	Cost per cost driver
Set-up costs	10,000	Number of set-ups	5	2,000.00
Rent and power (production area)	120,000	Number of wks' production	50	2,400.00
Rent (stores area)	50,000	Floor area of Stores (m^2)	800	62.50
Salaries of store issue staff	40,000	No of issues of inventory (stock)	10,000	4.00
	220,000			

Step 2. Reallocation of overheads based on costs per cost driver

Server	(i)	(ii)	(i) × (ii)
	Number of cost drivers	Cost per cost driver	Allocated overheads
		£	£
Set-up costs	5	2,000.00	10,000
Rent and power (production area)	10	2,400.00	24,000
Rent (stores area)	400	62.50	25,000
Salaries of store issue staff	2,000	4.00	8,000
			67,000

PC	(i)	(ii)	(i) × (ii)
	Number of cost drivers	Cost per cost driver	Allocated overheads
		£	£
Set-up costs	0	2,000.00	–
Rent and power (production area)	40	2,400.00	96,000
Rent (stores area)	400	62.50	25,000
Salaries of store issue staff	8,000	4.00	32,000
			153,000

Task 2.9

	Plastic allocated overheads – £	Metal allocated overheads – £
Power for machinery	50,000	60,000
Rent of factory	100,000	20,000
Canteen costs	32,000	8,000
Total overheads	182,000	88,000

Workings

Calculation of cost per cost driver

	Budgeted overheads	Cost driver	Number of cost drivers	Cost per cost driver
Power for machinery	110,000	Number of machine hours	5,500	20
Rent of factory	120,000	Floor space	1,200	100
Canteen costs	40,000	Number of employees	250	160

Reallocation of overheads based on costs per cost driver

Plastic	(i)	(ii)	(i) × (ii)
	Number of cost drivers	Cost per cost driver	Allocated overheads
		£	£
	2,500	20	50,000
Rent of factory	1,000	100	100,000
	200	160	32,000
			<u>182,000</u>

Answer bank

Metal

	(i)	(ii)	(i) × (ii)
	Number of cost drivers	*Cost per cost driver*	*Allocated overheads*
		£	£
		20	60,000
	200	100	20,000
	50	160	8,000
			88,000

....

Chapter 3

Task 3.1

The break even point in units is 100,000 units

The margin of safety in units is 15,000 units

The margin of safety as a percentage of budgeted sales is 13%

Workings

Breakeven point $= \dfrac{£1,100,000}{£28 - £17}$

$\qquad\qquad = 100,000$ units

Margin of safety (units) = Budgeted sales – breakeven sales

$\qquad\qquad\qquad = (115,000 - 100,000)$ units

$\qquad\qquad\qquad = 15,000$ units

Margin of safety (% budgeted sales) $= \dfrac{115,000 - 100,000}{115,000} \times 100\%$

$\qquad\qquad\qquad\qquad = 13\%$

....

Task 3.2

B

Workings

Contribution per unit = £(16 – 8) = £8

Contribution required to breakeven = fixed costs = £40,000

Breakeven point $= \dfrac{\text{Fixed costs}}{\text{Contribution per unit}}$

$\qquad\qquad = \dfrac{£40,000}{£8}$

$\qquad\qquad = 5,000$ units

Sales revenue at breakeven point = 5,000 units × £16 per unit

$\qquad\qquad\qquad\qquad = £80,000$

....

Task 3.3

D

Workings

Margin of safety = Budgeted sales volume – breakeven sales volume

Breakeven sales volume = $\dfrac{\text{Fixed costs}}{\text{Contribution per unit}}$

$= \dfrac{£110,000}{£55}$

= 2,000 units

Therefore, margin of safety (units) = 2,500 units – 2,000 units

= 500 units

Therefore, margin of safety (sales revenue) = margin of safety (units) × selling price per unit

= 500 units × £80

= £40,000

....

Task 3.4

The number of units of the product that the business must sell in order to make a target profit of £300,000 is 46,667 units

Workings

Target profit units = $\dfrac{£540,000 + £300,000}{£83 - 65}$

= 46,667 units

....

Task 3.5

The sales revenue required in order to make a target profit of £250,000 is £2,560,000

Workings

Profit volume ratio = $\dfrac{£40 - 28}{£40} \times 100\%$

= 30%

Target profit sales revenue = $\dfrac{£518,000 + £250,000}{0.3}$

= £2,560,000

....

Task 3.6

Product	Units
B	800
A	1,000
C	50

Workings

Contribution per kg

	A	*B*	*C*
Contribution	£12	£16	£16
Kg per unit	2	1	4
Contribution per kg	£6	£16	£4
Ranking	2	1	3

Production plan

	Units	*Kg used*	*Cumulative kg used*
B	800	800	800
A	1,000	2,000	2,800
C (balance)	50	<u>200</u>	3,000
		3,000	

....

Task 3.7

Product	Units
T	8,000
R	20,000
S	12,000

The contribution that will be earned under this production plan is £540,000

Workings

Identify the limiting factor

Materials – at maximum demand

$(4 \times 20,000) + (5 \times 25,000) + (3 \times 8,000) = 229,000$ kg

Labour hours – at maximum demand

$(2 \times 20,000) + (3 \times 25,000) + (3 \times 8,000) = 139,000$ hours

Machine hours – at maximum demand

$(4 \times 20,000) + (3 \times 25,000) + (2 \times 8,000) = 171,000$ hours

Therefore the only limiting factor is labour hours.

Contribution per labour hour

	R	S	T
Contribution	£11	£14	£19
Labour hours	2	3	3
Contribution per labour hour	£5.50	£4.67	£6.33
Ranking	2	3	1

Production plan

	Units	Labour hours used	Cumulative labour hours used
T	8,000	24,000	24,000
R	20,000	40,000	64,000
S (balance)	12,000	36,000	100,000
		100,000	

Contribution earned

	£
R (20,000 × £11)	220,000
S (12,000 × £14)	168,000
T (8,000 × £19)	152,000
	540,000

Task 3.8

The net present value of the investment is £(5,682)

Workings

Net present value

Year	Cash flow £	Discount factor @ 7%	Present value £
0	(84,000)	1.000	(84,000)
1	26,000	0.935	24,310
2	30,000	0.873	26,190
3	21,000	0.816	17,136
4	14,000	0.763	10,682
Net present value			(5,682)

Task 3.9

The net present value of the potential investment is £41,591

Workings

Net present value

Year	Cash flow	Discount factor	Present value
	£	@ 12%	£
0	(355,000)	1.000	(355,000)
1 (47 + 60)	107,000	0.893	95,551
2 (55 + 60)	115,000	0.797	91,655
3 (68 + 60)	128,000	0.712	91,136
4 (53 + 60)	113,000	0.635	71,755
5 (22 + 60)	82,000	0.567	46,494
Net present value			41,591

Note that depreciation is not a cash flow and having been charged in arriving at the profit figure must be added back to find the cash inflow in each year.

Task 3.10

			Terminal value at time 3
Cash inflow at time 1	£90,000 x 1.07 x 1.07	=	£103,041
Cash inflow at time 2	£130,000 x 1.07	=	£139,100
Cash inflow at time 3		=	£70,000
			£312,141
Less: initial outflow (£200,000 x 1.07 x 1.07 x 1.07)			(£245,009)
Net terminal value			£67,132

Chapter 4

Task 4.1

	Production costs	Three month moving total	Three month moving average
	£	£	£
March	104,500		
April	110,300	327,600	109,200
May	112,800	332,500	110,833
June	109,400	339,800	113,267
July	117,600	343,000	114,333
August	116,000	352,800	117,600
September	119,200	357,500	119,167
October	122,300	362,000	120,667
November	120,500	362,100	120,700
December	119,300		

Task 4.2

		Actual	5-day moving average TREND	Seasonal variation (actual – trend)
		£	£	£
Week 1	Day 1	600		
	Day 2	700		
	Day 3	1,000	1,000	–
	Day 4	1,200	1,016	+184
	Day 5	1,500	1,026	+474
Week 2	Day 1	680	1,076	–396
	Day 2	750	1,116	–366
	Day 3	1,250	1,188	+ 62
	Day 4	1,400	1,216	+184
	Day 5	1,860	1,272	+588
Week 3	Day 1	820	1,410	–590
	Day 2	1,030	1,550	–520
	Day 3	1,940	1,678	+262
	Day 4	2,100	1,714	+386
	Day 5	2,500	1,772	+728
Week 4	Day 1	1,000	1,696	–696
	Day 2	1,320	1,734	–414
	Day 3	1,560	1,768	–208
	Day 4	2,290		
	Day 5	2,670		

Task 4.3

(i)

		Actual	4-quarter moving average	Centred moving average – TREND	Seasonal variations
		£	£	£	£
20X5	Quarter 3	50,600			
	Quarter 4	52,800			
			51,900		
20X6	Quarter 1	55,600		51,975	+3,625
			52,050		
	Quarter 2	48,600		52,188	–3,588
			52,325		
	Quarter 3	51,200		52,625	–1,425
			52,925		
	Quarter 4	53,900		53,075	+825
			53,225		
20X7	Quarter 1	58,000		53,450	+4,550
			53,675		
	Quarter 2	49,800		53,763	–3,963
			53,850		
	Quarter 3	53,000		54,113	–1,113
			54,375		
	Quarter 4	54,600		54,488	+112
			54,600		
20X8	Quarter 1	60,100		54,750	+5,350
			54,900		
	Quarter 2	50,700		54,975	–4,275
			55,050		
	Quarter 3	54,200			
	Quarter 4	55,200			

(ii)   Seasonal variations

	Quarter 1	Quarter 2	Quarter 3	Quarter 4
	£	£	£	£
20X6	+3,625	−3,588	−1,425	+825
20X7	+4,550	−3,963	−1,113	+112
20X8	+5,350	−4,275		
	+13,525	−11,826	−2,538	+937
Average	+4,508	−3,942	−1,269	+469
Difference *				
234/4	+59	+59	+58	+58
	+4,567	−3,883	−1,211	+527

* Sum of averages = -234, so need to add back 234 to get the total seasonal variation to zero.

••

Task 4.4

Predicted sales

		£
Quarter 1	£418,500 + £21,500	440,000
Quarter 2	£420,400 + £30,400	450,800
Quarter 3	£422,500 − £16,700	405,800
Quarter 4	£423,800 − £35,200	388,600

••

Task 4.5

(a)

	Actual costs	RPI	Workings	Costs at January prices
	£			£
January	129,600	171.1	129,600	129,600
February	129,700	172.0	129,700 x 171.1/172.0	129,021
March	130,400	172.2	130,400 x 171.1/172.2	129,567
April	131,600	173.0	131,600 x 171.1/173.0	130,155
May	130,500	174.1	130,500 x 171.1/174.1	128,251
June	131,600	174.3	131,600 x 171.1/174.3	129,184

(b)

	Actual costs	RPI	Workings	Costs at June prices
	£			£
January	129,600	171.1	129,600 x 174.3/171.1	132,024
February	129,700	172.0	129,700 x 174.3/172.0	131,434
March	130,400	172.2	130,400 x 174.3/172.2	131,990
April	131,600	173.0	131,600 x 174.3/173.0	132,589
May	130,500	174.1	130,500 x 174.3/174.1	130,650
June	131,600	174.3	131,600 x 174.3/174.3	131,600

Task 4.6

		Sales		Index
		£		
20X7	Quarter 1	126,500		100.0
	Quarter 2	130,500	130,500/126,500 x 100	103.2
	Quarter 3	131,400	131,400/126,500 x 100	103.9
	Quarter 4	132,500	132,500/126,500 x 100	104.7
20X8	Quarter 1	133,100	133,100/126,500 x 100	105.2
	Quarter 2	135,600	135,600/126,500 x 100	107.2
	Quarter 3	136,500	136,500/126,500 x 100	107.9
	Quarter 4	137,100	137,100/126,500 x 100	108.4

Task 4.7

The updated standard cost for material C is £4.41

Working

£3.50 x 145/115 = £4.41

Task 4.8

Quarter 1 £667,396

Quarter 2 £722,633

Workings

Quarter 1   £657,000 x 128.4/126.4   =   £667,396

Quarter 2   £692,500 x 131.9/126.4   =   £722,633

Task 4.9

a is £2,000

b is £5

If production is 750 units, the cost of production is £5,750.

Workings

100 units

£2,500 = a + (100 x b)

1,000 units

£7,000 = a + (1,000 x b)

Subtracting the two equations gives:

£(7,000 – 2,500) = a + (1,000 x b) – a – (100 x b)

£4,500 = 900 x b

b = 5

Substituting b = 5 into the first equation gives:

£2,500 = a + (100 x 5)

£2,500 = a + £500

a = £2,000

Production costs   =   2,000 + (5 x 750)

                               =   £5,750

Note that this is similar to hi-lo technique of finding the variable and fixed elements. of a semi-variable cost, if the activity levels given are assumed to be the highest and lowest.

100 units   £2,500

1,000 units   £7,000

Subtract the highest less the lowest activities to find the variable cost which is b in the equation:

1,000 – 100 = 900 units with additional cost of £(7,000 – 2,500) = £4,500, ie £4,500/900 per unit = £5 per unit

b = £5

Therefore, to find the fixed cost element, consider 100 units:

Fixed costs = total costs – variable costs

= £2,500 – 5 x 100

= £2,000

so a = £2,000

Task 4.10

If production is expected to be 105,000 units in the next quarter the anticipated production costs are £810,000

Workings

Production costs = 138,000 + (6.4 x 105,000)

= £810,000

....

Task 4.11

The anticipated power costs for April are £270,000.

Working

Power costs 80,000 + (380,000 x 0.5) = £270,000

....

Task 4.12

Month 1	25,600 units
Month 2	26,500 units
Month 3	27,400 units

Workings

Month 1: sales trend = 3.1 + (0.9 x 25) (month 25)

= 25,600 units

Month 2: sales trend = 3.1 + (0.9 x 26)

= 26,500 units

Month 3: sales trend = 3.1 + (0.9 x 27)

= 27,400 units

....

Task 4.13

Quarter 1	1,590 units
Quarter 2	2,095 units
Quarter 3	2,125 units
Quarter 4	1,880 units

Workings

	Trend		*Seasonal variation*		*Estimate of actual*
Quarter 1	400 + (105) x 13	=	1,765 – 175	=	1,590
Quarter 2	400 + (105) x 14	=	1,870 + 225	=	2,095
Quarter 3	400 + (105) x 15	=	1,975 + 150	=	2,125
Quarter 4	400 + (105) x 16	=	2,080 – 200	=	1,880

....

Chapter 5

Task 5.1

MEMORANDUM

To: New Accounts Assistant

From: Accountant

Date: xx/xx/xx

Subject: **Setting the standard cost of labour**

The standard cost of the direct labour for a product will be made up of:

* the amount of time being spent on each unit of the product
* the hourly wage rate for the employees working on the product

  Factors that should be taken into account when setting the standard for the amount of labour time include:

* the level of skill or training of the labour used on the product
* any anticipated changes in the grade of labour used on the product
* any anticipated changes in work methods or productivity levels
* the effect on productivity of any bonus scheme to be introduced

  The hourly rate for the direct labour used on the product can be found from the payroll records. However consideration should be given to:

* anticipated pay rises
* any anticipated changes in the grade of labour to be used
* the effect of any bonus scheme on the labour rate
* whether any overtime is anticipated and should be built into the hourly rate

Task 5.2

	Variance - £	Adverse/Favourable
Total materials cost variance	4,480	Adverse
Materials price variance	2,880	Adverse
Materials usage variance	1,600	Adverse

Workings

(i)   Total materials cost variance

	£
Standard cost of actual production 2,800 units x 5 kg x £4.00	56,000
Actual cost	60,480
Total cost variance	4,480 (A)

(ii)   Materials price variance

	£
Actual quantity at standard cost 14,400 kg x £4.00	57,600
Actual cost	60,480
Price variance	2,880 (A)

(iii)   Materials usage variance

	£
Standard quantity at standard cost 2,800 units x 5 kg x £4.00	56,000
Actual quantity at standard cost 14,400 kg x £4.00	57,600
Usage variance	1,600 (A)

....

Task 5.3

	Variance £	Adverse/Favourable
Total materials cost variance	13,680	Adverse
Materials price variance	16,080	Adverse
Materials usage variance	2,400	Favourable

Workings

(i)   Total materials cost variance

	£
Standard cost for actual production 11,400 units x 4 kg x £3	136,800
Actual cost	150,480
Total cost variance	13,680 (A)

(ii)   Materials price variance

	£
Actual quantity at standard cost 44,800 kg x £3	134,400
Actual cost	150,480
Price variance	16,080 (A)

(iii)   Materials usage variance

	£
Standard quantity at standard cost 11,400 units x 4 kg x £3	136,800
Actual quantity at standard cost 44,800 kg x £3	134,400
Usage variance	2,400 (F)

....

Task 5.4

	Variance £	Adverse/Favourable
Total labour cost variance	12,715	Adverse
Labour rate variance	9,430	Adverse
Labour efficiency variance	3,285	Adverse

Workings

(i) Total labour cost variance

	£
Standard cost for actual production 12,100 units x 4.5 hours x £7.30	397,485
Actual cost	410,200
Total cost variance	12,715 (A)

(ii) Labour rate variance

	£
Actual hours at standard rate 54,900 x £7.30	400,770
Actual hours at actual cost	410,200
Rate variance	9,430 (A)

(iii) Labour efficiency variance

	£
Standard hours at standard rate 12,100 units x 4.5 hours x £7.30	397,485
Actual hours at standard rate 54,900 x £7.30	400,770
Efficiency variance	3,285 (A)

....

Task 5.5

	Variance £	Adverse/Favourable
Total labour cost variance	2,200	Favourable
Labour rate variance	4,200	Favourable
Labour efficiency variance	2,000	Adverse

Workings

(i) Total labour cost variance

	£
Standard cost for actual production 10,680 units x 5 hours x £10	534,000
Actual cost	531,800
Total cost variance	2,200 (F)

(ii) Labour rate variance

	£
Actual hours at standard rate 53,600 x £10	536,000
Actual hours at actual cost	531,800
Rate variance	4,200 (F)

(iii) Labour efficiency variance

	£
Standard hours at standard rate 10,680 units x 5 hours x £10	534,000
Actual hours at standard rate 53,600 x £10	536,000
Efficiency variance	2,000 (A)

Task 5.6

	Variance £	Adverse/Favourable
Total labour cost variance	8,600	Adverse
Labour rate variance	4,100	Adverse
Labour efficiency variance	4,500	Adverse

Workings

(i) Total labour cost variance

	£
Standard cost for actual production 11,400 x 3 hours x £9	307,800
Actual cost	316,400
Total variance	8,600 (A)

(ii)   Labour rate variance

	£
Actual hours at standard rate 34,700 hours x £9	312,300
Actual cost	316,400
Rate variance	4,100 (A)

(iii)   Labour efficiency variance

	£
Standard hours at standard rate 11,400 units x 3 hours x £9	307,800
Actual hours at standard rate 34,700 hours x £9	312,300
Efficiency variance	4,500 (A)

Task 5.7

The fixed overhead expenditure variance is £5,000 Adverse

The fixed overhead volume variance is £10,500 Favourable

Workings

(i)   Fixed overhead expenditure variance

	£
Budgeted overhead £7 x 10,000 units	70,000
Actual overhead	75,000
Expenditure variance	5,000 (A)

(ii)   Fixed overhead volume variance

	£
Actual production @ standard OAR 11,500 x £7	80,500
Budgeted production @ standard OAR 10,000 x £7	70,000
Volume variance	10,500 (F)

Task 5.8

	Variance £	Adverse/Favourable
Fixed overhead expenditure variance	80,000	Favourable
Fixed overhead volume variance	91,200	Favourable
Fixed overhead efficiency variance	15,200	Favourable
Fixed overhead capacity variance	76,000	Favourable

Workings

Fixed overhead expenditure variance

	£
Budgeted fixed overhead 50,000 units x 6 hours x £7.60	2,280,000
Actual fixed overhead	2,200,000
Expenditure variance	80,000 (F)

Fixed overhead volume variance

	£
Standard hours for actual production @ standard OAR 52,000 units x 6 hours x £7.60	2,371,200
Standard hours for budgeted production @ standard OAR 50,000 units x 6 hours x £7.60	2,280,000
Volume variance	91,200 (F)

Fixed overhead efficiency variance

	£
Standard hours for actual production @ standard OAR 52,000 x 6 hours x £7.60	2,371,200
Actual hours @ standard OAR 310,000 x £7.60	2,356,000
Efficiency variance	15,200 (F)

Fixed overhead capacity variance

	£
Actual hours @ standard OAR 310,000 x £7.60	2,356,000
Budgeted hours @ standard OAR 50,000 x 6 x £7.60	2,280,000
Capacity variance	76,000 (F)

Task 5.9

(i)   The budgeted fixed overhead for the month was £201,600

(ii) The fixed overhead expenditure variance was £1,400 Adverse

(iii) The fixed overhead volume variance was £11,520 Adverse

(iv) The fixed overhead efficiency variance was £10,080 Favourable

(v)   The fixed overhead capacity variance was £21,600 Adverse

Workings

(i)

	£
Budgeted fixed overhead 14,000 units x 4 hours x £3.60	201,600

(ii)   Fixed overhead expenditure variance

	£
Budgeted fixed overhead	201,600
Actual fixed overhead	203,000
Expenditure variance	1,400 (A)

(iii) Fixed overhead volume variance

	£
Standard hours for actual production @ standard OAR 13,200 units x 4 hours x £3.60	190,080
Standard hours for budgeted production @ standard OAR 14,000 units x 4 hours x £3.60	201,600
Volume variance	11,520 (A)

(iv) Fixed overhead efficiency variance

	£
Standard hours for actual production @ standard OAR 13,200 x 4 hours x £3.60	190,080
Actual hours @ standard OAR 50,000 x £3.60	180,000
Efficiency variance	10,080 (F)

(v)   Fixed overhead capacity variance

	£
Actual hours @ standard OAR 50,000 x £3.60	180,000
Budgeted hours @ standard OAR 14,000 x 4 x £3.60	201,600
Capacity variance	21,600 (A)

Task 5.10

	Adverse £	Favourable £	Total £
Budgeted cost of actual production 1,240 x £38.69			47,976
Variances			
Materials price	860		
Materials usage		426	
Labour rate		820	
Labour efficiency	1,530		
Fixed overhead expenditure	250		
Fixed overhead efficiency	288		
Fixed overhead capacity		848	
Total variances	2928	2094	834
Actual cost of actual production (17,100 + 27,060 + 4,650)			48,810

···

Task 5.11

D

	£	£
Materials		
A 1.2 kg × £11 =	13.20	
B 4.7 kg × £6 =	28.20	
		41.40
Labour		
1.5 hours × £8		12.00
Prime cost		53.40
Overheads		
1.5 hours × £30		45.00
Standard cost per unit		98.40

···

Task 5.12

D

Budgeted fixed overhead absorption rate = £22,260 ÷ 8,400 hours = £2.65 per labour hour

Budgeted hours of work	8,400 hrs
Actual hours of work	7,980 hrs
	420 hrs (A
× standard rate per hour	× £2.65
Fixed production overhead capacity variance	£1,113 (A)

··

Task 5.13

A   Neither fixed overhead efficiency variance nor fixed overhead capacity variance (which together make up the fixed overhead volume variance) exist in a marginal costing system.

··

Task 5.14

(a) (i)

Budgeted fixed overhead expenditure (4,100 × 40 × £12.50)	2,050,000
Actual fixed overhead expenditure	2,195,000
Fixed overhead **expenditure variance**	145,000 (A)

(ii)

	£
Actual production at standard rate (3,850 × 40 × £12.50)	1,925,000
Budgeted production at standard rate (4,100 × 40 × £12.50)	2,050,000
Fixed overhead **volume variance**	125,000 (A)

(iii)

Budgeted hours (4,100 × 40)	164,000 hrs
Actual hours	159,000 hrs
Fixed overhead capacity variance in hours	5,000 hrs (A)
× standard rate per hour	× £12.50
Fixed overhead **capacity variance**	£62,500 (A)

(iv)

3,850 units should have taken (× 40 hrs)	154,000 hrs
but did take	159,000 hrs
Fixed overhead efficiency variance in hours	5,000 hrs (A)
× standard rate per hour	× £12.50
Fixed overhead **efficiency variance**	£62,500 (A)

(b) REPORT

To: Production Director

From: Assistant Management Accountant

Date: xx/xx/xx

Subject: **Fixed overhead variances**

This memorandum provides information on fixed overhead variances. In particular it covers the similarities between fixed overhead variances and other cost variances, the meaning of the various fixed overhead variances and the ways in which such variances can be of assistance in the planning and the controlling of the division.

Similarities between fixed overhead variances and other variances

The fixed overhead expenditure variance is the difference between the budgeted fixed overhead expenditure and actual fixed overhead expenditure. It is therefore similar to the material price and labour rate variances in that it shows the effect on costs and hence profit of paying more or less than anticipated for resources used.

Material usage and labour efficiency variances show the effect on costs and hence profit of having used more or less resource than should have been used for the actual volume of production. Fixed overheads should remain constant within the relevant range of production, however; they should not change simply because budgeted and actual production volumes differ. Fixed overhead variances similar to material usage and labour efficiency variances (reflecting the difference between the actual fixed overhead expenditure and the fixed overhead expenditure which should have been incurred at the actual volume of production) cannot therefore occur.

The meaning of fixed overhead variances

Whereas labour and material total variances show the effect on costs and hence profit of the difference between what the actual production volume should have cost and what it did cost (in terms of labour or material), if an organisation uses standard absorption costing (as we do), the fixed overhead total variance is the difference between actual fixed overhead expenditure and the fixed overhead absorbed (the under- or over-absorbed overhead).

The total under- or over-absorption is made up of the fixed overhead expenditure variance and the fixed overhead volume variance. The volume variance shows that part of the under- or over-absorbed overhead which is due to any difference between budgeted production volume and actual production volume.

The volume variance can be further broken down into an efficiency variance and a capacity variance. The capacity variance shows how much of the under- or over-absorbed overhead is due to working the labour force or plant more or less than planned, whereas the efficiency variance shows the effect of the efficiency of the labour force or plant.

The volume variance and its two subdivisions, the efficiency variance and the capacity variance, measure the extent of under or over absorption due to production volume being different to that planned. Material usage and labour efficiency variances, on the other hand, measure the effect of usage being different from that expected for the actual volume achieved.

Fixed overhead variances and planning and control

The fixed overhead volume variance and its subdivisions are perhaps misleading as variances for management control, because unlike expenditure variances or variable cost efficiency variances, they are not a true reflection of the extra or lower cash spending by an organisation as a result of the variance occurring. However, the fixed overhead efficiency and capacity variances are of some relevance for planning and control. They provide some measure of the difference between budgeted production volume and actual production volume, and management should obviously be interested in whether budgeted output was achieved, and if not, why not. A favourable efficiency variance might indicate an efficient workforce whereas an unfavourable capacity variance might indicate plant breakdowns or strikes. The existence of a fixed overhead volume variance can therefore be important; it is only the monetary value given to it that can be misleading.

The fixed overhead expenditure variance highlights the effect on costs and hence profit of changes to the level of overheads. For overhead expenditure variances to have any practical value as a planning or control measure, the variance for each overhead cost centre needs to be calculated, and reported to the manager responsible. Within each overhead cost centre, the manager should be able to analyse the total variance into indirect material cost variances, indirect labour cost variances and excess or favourable spending on other items, such as depreciation, postage, telephone charges and so on. Managers can then, for example, consider other suppliers, reconsider pricing structures of products and the like.

****

Task 5.15

The correct answer is the work in progress control account.

****

Task 5.16

(a) (1) Standard price of fuel = £497,664/1,244,160 litres = £0.40 per litre.

(2) Standard litres of fuel per crossing = 1,244,160/6,480 = 192 litres

Standard litres of fuel for 5,760 crossings = 192 × 5,760 = 1,105,920 litres

(3) Standard labour rate per hr = £699,840/93,312 hrs = £7.50 per hour

(4) Standard labour hours per crossing = 93,312/6,480 = 14.4 hours

Standard labour hours for 5,760 crossings = 14.4 × 5,760 = 82,944 hours

(5) Standard fixed overhead cost per budgeted operating hour = £466,560/7,776 = £60 per hour

(6) Standard operating hours per crossing = 7,776/6,480 = 1.2 hours

Standard operating hours for 5,760 crossings = 1.2 × 5,760 = 6,912 hours

(7) Standard fixed overhead cost absorbed by 5,760 crossings = 6,912 hours (6) × £60 per hour (from (5)) = £414,720

(b)   (1)

		£
1,232,800 litres should cost (× £0.40 (a)(i)(1))		493,120
but did cost		567,088
Material price variance for fuel		73,968 (A)

(2)

		£	
5,760 crossings should have used (a)i)2))		1,105,920	litres
but did use		1,232,800	litres
Usage variance in litres		126,880	litres (A)
× standard price per litre (a)i)1))		× £0.40	
Material usage variance for fuel		£50,752	(A)

(3)

		£
89,856 hours should have cost (× £7.50 a)i)3))		673,920
but did cost		696,384
Labour rate variance		22,464 (A)

(4)

5,760 crossings should have used (a)i)4))		82,944	hours
but did take		89,856	hours
Efficiency variance in hours		6,912	hours (A)
× standard rate per hours (a)i)3))		× £7.50	
Labour efficiency variance		£51,840	(A)

(5)

		£
Budgeted fixed overhead expenditure		466,560
Actual fixed overhead expenditure		472,440
Fixed overhead expenditure variance		5,800 (A)

(6)

		£
Actual number of crossings (5,760) at standard rate (a)i)7))		414,720
Budgeted number of crossings at standard rate		466,560 (A)
Fixed overhead volume variance		51,840

(7)

Budgeted operating hours		7,776
Actual operating hours		7,488
Capacity variance in hours		288 (A)
× std fixed o/hd cost per operating hours (a)i)5))		× £60
Fixed overhead capacity variance		£17,280 (A)

(8)

5,760 crossings should take (a)i)6))		6,912	operating hours
but did take		7,488	operating hours
Efficiency variance in operating hours		576	operating hours (A)
× std fixed o/hd cost per op hr (a)i)5))	× £60		
Fixed overhead efficiency variance	£34,560	(A)	

(c) **Statement reconciling the actual cost of operations to the standard cost of operations for year ended 30 November 20X8**

	£	£
Number of ferry crossings		5,760
Actual cost of operations		1,735,912
Cost variances	*Adverse*	
Material price for fuel	73,968	
Material usage for fuel	50,752	
Labour rate	22,464	
Labour efficiency	51,840	
Fixed overhead expenditure	5,880	
Fixed overhead capacity	17,280	
Fixed overhead efficiency	34,560	
		256,744 (A)
Standard cost of operations		1,479,168*

* Check. 5,760/6,480 × £1,664,064 = £1,479,168

Chapter 6

Task 6.1

Variance	Possible causes
Favourable materials price variance	• negotiation of a better price from a supplier • negotiation of a trade or bulk purchase discount from a supplier • purchase of a lower grade of materials
Favourable materials usage variance	• use of a higher grade of material which led to less wastage • use of more skilled labour leading to less wastage than normal • new machinery which provides greater efficiency
Adverse labour rate variance	• unexpected increase in labour costs • use of a higher grade of labour than anticipated • unexpectedly high levels of overtime
Adverse labour efficiency variance	• use of a less skilled grade of labour • use of a lower grade of material which takes longer to work on • more idle time than budgeted for • poor supervision of the workforce • problems with machinery

Task 6.2

Scenario	Possible effects
A business has had to use a less-skilled grade of labour in its production process	• Favourable labour rate variance • Adverse labour efficiency variance • Adverse materials usage variance
A factory had a machine breakdown which resulted in three days of production delays last month.	• Adverse labour efficiency variance • Adverse fixed overhead expenditure variance (due to additional costs of mending the machine) • Adverse fixed overhead volume variance • Adverse fixed overhead efficiency variance • Adverse fixed overhead capacity variance

Task 6.3

New warehouse – this will have the effect of simply reducing the fixed overhead expense (assuming the rent saved exceeds any new depreciation charge) and therefore is part of the favourable fixed overhead expenditure variance. The standard fixed overhead cost should be adjusted to reflect the rental saving.

New machines – the new machines use less power than the old ones therefore reducing the power costs element of the fixed overhead. The additional depreciation charge however will increase the fixed overhead expense. Once the reduction in power costs and increase in depreciation charge are known then the standard fixed overhead should be adjusted.

Price increase – the price increase will be a cause of the adverse materials price variance. The price increase appears to be a permanent one as all suppliers have increased their prices, so the standard materials cost should be altered.

Skilled labour – the use of the higher skilled labour will have been part of the cause of the favourable labour efficiency variance and the favourable materials usage variance. If the fixed overheads are absorbed on a labour hour basis then the efficiency of the skilled labour will also be a cause of the favourable fixed overhead efficiency variance. The additional expense of the skilled labour and the overtime that has been worked will have been causes of the adverse labour rate variance. The overtime may also have led to the favourable capacity variance as actual hours exceeded the budgeted hours. Unless the use of this grade of labour is likely to be a permanent policy, then there should be no change to the standard labour rate or hours.

Task 6.4

The total materials price variance is £36,600 Adverse

The planning element of the materials price variance that has been caused by the price increase is £22,550 Adverse

The control element of the materials price variance caused by other factors is £14,050 Adverse

Workings

Total materials price variance

	£
Standard cost for actual quantity 45,100 x £8	360,800
Actual cost	397,400
	36,600 (A)

Planning variance caused by price increase

	£
Standard cost for actual quantity 45,100 x £8	360,800
Adjusted cost for actual quantity 45,100 x £8.50	383,350
	22,550 (A)

Control variance caused by other factors

	£
Adjusted cost for actual quantity 45,100 x £8.50	383,350
Actual cost	397,400
	14,050 (A)

....

Task 6.5

The total materials price variance is £4,240 Adverse

The planning variance due to price increase is £5,300 Adverse

The control variance due to other factors is £1,060 Favourable

Workings

Total materials price variance

	£
Standard cost of actual quantity 10,600 x £6.50	68,900
Actual cost	73,140
	4,240 (A)

Planning variance due to price increase

	£
Standard cost of actual quantity 10,600 x £6.50	68,900
Price adjusted cost of actual quantity 10,600 x £7.00	74,200
	5,300 (A)

Control variance due to other factors

	£
Price adjusted cost of actual quantity 10,600 x £7.00	74,200
Actual cost	73,140
	1,060 (F)

....

Task 6.6

The total materials price variance is £12,800 Favourable

The planning variance due to the season is £38,640 Favourable

The control variance due to other factors is £25,840 Adverse

Workings

Total materials price variance

	£
Standard cost of actual quantity 92,000 x £7.00	644,000
Actual cost	631,200
	12,800 (F)

Planning variance due to season

	£
Standard cost of actual quantity 92,000 x £7.00	644,000
Seasonally adjusted price 92,000 x (£7.00 - £0.42)	605,360
	38,640 (F)

Control variance due to other factors

	£
Seasonally adjusted price 92,000 x (£7.00 - £0.42)	605,360
Actual cost	631,200
	25,840 (A)

Task 6.7

The total materials price variance is £25,380 Adverse

The planning variance caused by the seasonal price change is £30,456 Adverse

The control variance caused by other factors is £5,076 Favourable

Workings

Total materials cost variance

	£
Standard cost of actual quantity 42,300 x £4.00	169,200
Actual cost	194,580
	25,380 (A)

Planning variance due to season

	£
Standard cost of actual quantity 42,300 x £4.00	169,200
Seasonally adjusted cost 42,300 x (£4.00 + £0.72)	199,656
	30,456 (A)

Control variance due to other factors

	£
Seasonally adjusted cost 42,300 x (£4.00 + £0.72)	199,656
Actual cost	194,580
	5,076 (F)

....

Task 6.8

The total materials price variance is £26,000 Adverse

The planning variance caused by the index change is £76,667 Adverse

The control variance caused by other factors is £50,667 Favourable

Workings

Total materials cost variance

	£
Standard cost of actual quantity 46,000 x £20	920,000
Actual cost	946,000
	26,000 (A)

Planning variance due to index change

	£
Standard cost of actual quantity 46,000 x £20	920,000
Index adjusted cost 46,000 x £20 x 130/120	996,667
	76,667 (A)

Control variance due to other factors

	£
Index adjusted cost 46,000 x £20 x 130/120	996,667
Actual cost	946,000
	50,667 (F)

....

Task 6.9

(a) **MEMO**

To: Managing Director
From: Assistant Management Accountant
Date: xx/xx/xx
Subject: The use of standard marginal costing at Finchley Ltd

As discussed at our earlier meetings, because all companies within the Hampstead Group use standard marginal costing, Finchley Ltd will need to adopt the system from 1 August 20X8. This report is intended to demonstrate and describe the use of standard marginal costing in your company.

(i) (1) **Standard marginal cost of a unit of Alpha**

	£
Material (36,000m ÷ 12,000) 3m × (£432,000 ÷ 36,000) £12 per m	36.00
Labour (72,000 hrs ÷ 12,000) 6 hrs × (£450,000 ÷ 72,000) £6.25 per hr	37.50
	73.50

(2) **Standard cost of producing 10,000 units of Alpha**

	£
Material (£36 × 10,000)	360,000
Labour (£37.50 × 10,000)	375,000
Standard marginal cost	735,000
Fixed overheads	396,000
Total cost	1,131,000

(ii) (1)

	£
32,000 m should have cost (× £12)	384,000
but did cost	377,600
Material price variance	6,400 (F)

(2)

10,000 units should have used (× 3 m)	30,000 m
but did use	32,000 m
Material usage variance in metres	2,000 m (A)
× standard cost per metre	× £12
Material usage variance in £	£24,000 (A)

(3)

	£
70,000 hrs should have cost (× £6.25)	437,500
but did cost	422,800
Labour rate variance	14,700 (F)

(4)

10,000 units should have taken (× 6 hrs)	60,000 hrs
but did take	70,000 hrs
Efficiency variance in hours	10,000 hrs (A)
× standard rate per hour	× £6.25
Labour efficiency variance in £	£62,500 (A)

(5)

	£
Budgeted fixed overhead expenditure	396,000
Actual fixed overhead expenditure (£330,000 + £75,000)	405,000
Fixed overhead expenditure variance	9,000 (A)

(iii) Set out below is a statement reconciling the standard cost of production for the three months ended 31 May 2008 with the actual cost of production for that period.

			£
Standard cost of output ((see (a)(i)(2))			1,131,000
Variances	*Adv*	*Fav*	
	£	£	
Material price		6,400	
Material usage	24,000		
Labour rate		14,700	
Labour efficiency	62,500		
Fixed overhead expenditure	9,000		
	95,500	21,100	74,400 (A)
Actual cost of output			1,205,400

(iv) The total labour variance in the statement above (£47,800 (A)) differs from that in your absorption costing management report for the three months ended 31 May 20X8 because the original report compares the actual cost of producing 10,000 units and the budgeted cost of producing 12,000 units. It therefore fails to compare like with like. The report above, however, compares actual costs of producing 10,000 units and what costs should have been given the actual output

of 10,000 units. The total material variances in the two reports also differ for this reason. There is very little point comparing a budgeted cost with an actual cost if the production level upon which the budgeted cost was based is not achieved.

The fixed overhead expenditure variance in the statement above also differs from the fixed overhead variance reported in the absorption costing statement. This is because the absorption costing statement compares overhead absorbed whereas the marginal costing statement compares overhead expenditure.

(v) There are other reasons why the reconciliation statement provides improved management information. (Note: only ONE is actually required)

(1) It separates total variances into their components and so you will be able to determine whether, for example, the total material variance is the responsibility of the purchasing manager (price variance) or the production manager (usage variance).

(2) It avoids the use of under-or over-absorbed overhead, which is simply a bookkeeping exercise and does not reflect higher or lower cash spending.

(3) It allows management by exception.

(4) The original statement conveys the wrong message (that the overall variance was favourable).

I hope this information has proved useful. If I can be of further assistance or you have any questions, please do not hesitate to contact me.

(b)

	(A) £	(F) £	£
Standard cost of output			1,131,000
Variances			
Labour rate due to machine breakdown (W1)		2,520	
Labour rate due to normal working (W1)		12,180	
Labour efficiency due to machine breakdown (W2)	75,000		
Labour efficiency due to normal working (W2)		12,500	
Material price due to change in price index (W3)		38,400	
Material price due to other reasons (W3)	32,000		
Material usage	24,000		
Fixed overhead expenditure	9,000	—	
	140,000	65,600	74,400 (A)
Actual cost of output			1,205,400

Answer bank

Workings

(1) £

    Total labour rate variance   14,700 (F)

    Labour rate variance due to machine breakdown
        (12,000/70,000 × £14,700)   2,520 (F)

    Labour rate variance due to normal working (balance)   12,180 (F)

Or:

£

Actual amount paid during breakdown   72,480
    (12,000 × £422,800/70,000)

Should have paid
    (12,000 × £6.25)   75,000

Labour rate variance due to breakdown   2,520 (F)

Labour rate variance due to normal working (balance)   12,180 (F)

(2) £

    Total labour efficiency variance   62,500 (A)

    Labour efficiency variance due to machine breakdown
        (12,000 hrs × £6.25)   75,000 (A)

    Labour efficiency variance due to normal production   12,500 (F)

(3) £   £

    Total material price variance   6,400 (F)

    Variance due to price index change 32,000 m
        should have cost (× £12 × 420.03/466.70)   345,600
    but should originally have cost (× £12)   384,000

     38,400 (F)

    Variance due to other reasons   32,000 (A)

Task 6.10

(a) (i) (1) Actual number of meals served = 4 meals × 7 days × 648 guests

= 18,144 meals

(2) Standard number of meals
for actual number of guests = 3 meals × 7 days × 648 guests

= 13,608 meals

(3) Actual hourly rate of pay = £5,280 ÷ 1,200 hours

= £4.40 per hour

(4) Standard hours allowed for
actual number of guests = (648 guests × 3 meals × 7 days)
÷ 12 meals per hour

= 1,134 hours

(5) Standard fixed overhead per guest = budgeted overheads ÷
budgeted number of guests

= £38,340 ÷ 540 = £71 per guest

(6) **Total standard cost for actual number of guests**

	£
Meal costs (13,608 meals × £3 per meal)	40,824
Catering staff costs (1,134 hours × £4 per hour)	4,536
Fixed overhead costs (648 × £71 per guest)	46,008
Total standard cost	91,368

(ii) (1)

	£
18,144 meals should cost (× £3)	54,432
but did cost	49,896
Material price variance for meals served	4,536 (F)

(2)

648 guests should have used (a)(i)(2))	13,608 meals
but did use (a)(i)(1))	18,144 meals
Usage variance in meals	4,536 meals (A)
× standard cost per meal	× £3
Material usage variance for meals served	£13,608 (A)

(3)

	£
1,200 hrs worked should have cost (× £4/hr)	4,800
but did cost	5,280
Labour rate variance for catering staff	480 (A)

(4)

Meals for 648 guests should have taken ((a)(i)(4))	1,134 hours
but did take	1,200 hours
Labour efficiency variance in hours	66 hours (A)
× standard rate per hour	× £4
Labour efficiency variance for catering staff	£264 (A)

(5)

	£
Budgeted fixed overhead expenditure	38,340
Actual fixed overhead expenditure	37,800
Fixed overhead expenditure variance	540 (F)

(6)

Actual number of guests	648
Budgeted number of guests	540
Volume variance – number of guests	108
× standard fixed overhead per guest ((a)(i)(5))	× £71
Fixed overhead volume variance	£7,668 (F)

(iii) **Bare Foot Hotel complex**

Standard cost reconciliation for seven days ended 27 November 20X8

Budgeted number of guests   540

Actual number of guests   648

	£		£	
Standard cost for 648 guests ((a)(i)(6))			91,368	
Cost variances				
Material price variance ((a)(ii)(1))	4,536	(F)		
Material usage variance ((a)(ii)(2))	13,608	(A)		
			9,072	(A)
Catering labour rate variance ((a)(ii)(3))	480	(A)		
Catering labour efficiency variance ((a)(ii)(4))	264	(A)		
			744	(A)
Fixed overhead expenditure variance ((a)(ii)(5))	540	(F)		
Fixed overhead volume variance ((a)(ii)(6))	7,668	(F)		
			8,208	(F)
Actual cost for 648 guests			92,976	

Note: (A) denotes adverse variance, (F) denotes favourable variance.

(b) **MEMO**

To: Alice Groves, general manager

From: Assistant management accountant

Date: xx.xx.xx

Subject: **Performance report** for seven days ended 27 November 20X8

This memorandum deals with a number of issues arising from the standard cost reconciliation statement prepared for the seven days ended 27 November 20X8.

(i) **Subdivision of the catering labour efficiency variance**

The adverse catering labour efficiency variance of £264 can be divided into that part due to guests taking more meals than planned and that part due to other efficiency reasons.

Standard hours allowed for 648 guests taking 3 meals ((a)(i)(4))	1,134 hours
Standard hours allowed for 648 guests taking 4 meals = (648 guests × 4 meals × 7 days) ÷ 12 meals per hour	1,512 hours
Excess hours due to guests taking more meals than planned	378 hours (A)
× standard rate per hour	× £4
Efficiency variance due to guests taking more meals than planned	£1,512 (A)
Standard hours allowed for 648 guests taking 4 meals (from above)	1,512 hours
Actual hours worked	1,200 hours
Efficiency variance due to other reasons (in hours)	312 hours (F)
× standard rate per hour	× £4
Catering labour efficiency variance due to other reasons	£1,248 (F)

(ii) **The meaning of the fixed overhead capacity and efficiency variances**

The fixed overhead absorption rate for our hotel is based on the budgeted overhead expenditure for the period, divided by the budgeted number of guests.

$$\text{Fixed overhead absorption rate} = \frac{\text{budgeted fixed overhead}}{\text{budgeted number of guests}}$$

If the actual overhead, or the actual number of guests, or both, are different from budget then over or under absorption of overhead may occur, so that there may be a fixed overhead variance.

A **volume variance** arises when the activity level is different from that budgeted, in our case if the actual number of guests is different from the budgeted number. In some organisations it may be possible to sub-divide the volume variance into two parts: the capacity variance and the efficiency variance.

The **capacity variance** arises when the utilisation of the available capacity is higher or lower than budgeted. It is usually calculated as the difference between budgeted and actual hours worked, multiplied by the fixed overhead absorption rate. Under or over utilisation of capacity can potentially lead to under– or over-absorbed overhead.

The **efficiency variance** arises when employees are working at a more or less efficient rate than standard to produce a given output. Producing output at a faster or slower rate could also potentially lead to under– or over-absorbed overhead.

(iii) **Calculating the fixed overhead capacity and efficiency variances for the Bare Foot Hotel complex**

The above descriptions of the fixed overhead capacity and efficiency variances highlight the need to be able to measure hours of work so that the volume variance can be subdivided.

It is not feasible to do this for the Bare Foot Hotel complex. We do have a measure of hours worked within the catering activity, but a large proportion of overheads are incurred on entertainment, for which we have no record of hours worked.

The absence of an activity measure based on hours worked therefore makes it difficult and meaningless to subdivide the fixed overhead volume variance into its capacity and efficiency elements.

Chapter 7

Task 7.1

	November	December	January	February
Actual hours per unit	1.53 hours	1.56 hours	1.45 hours	1.53 hours
Efficiency ratio	98.2%	96.3%	103.3%	98.2%
Capacity ratio	100.7%	110.1%	100.2%	98.9%
Activity ratio	98.9%	106.0%	103.5%	97.1%

Workings		*November*	*December*	*January*	*February*
(i)		$\dfrac{98,200}{64,300}$	$\dfrac{107,300}{68,900}$	$\dfrac{90,200}{62,100}$	$\dfrac{92,000}{60,200}$
	Actual hours per unit	1.53 hours per unit	1.56 hours per unit	1.45 hours per unit	1.53 hours per unit
(ii)		$\dfrac{64,300 \times 1.5}{98,200}$	$\dfrac{68,900 \times 1.5}{107,300}$	$\dfrac{62,100 \times 1.5}{90,200}$	$\dfrac{60,200 \times 1.5}{92,000}$
	Efficiency ratio	98.2%	96.3%	103.3%	98.2%
(iii)		$\dfrac{98,200}{65,000 \times 1.5}$	$\dfrac{107,300}{65,000 \times 1.5}$	$\dfrac{90,200}{60,000 \times 1.5}$	$\dfrac{92,000}{62,000 \times 1.5}$
	Capacity ratio	100.7%	110.1%	100.2%	98.9%
(iv)		$\dfrac{64,300}{65,000}$	$\dfrac{68,900}{65,000}$	$\dfrac{62,100}{60,000}$	$\dfrac{60,200}{62,000}$
	Activity ratio	98.9%	106.0%	103.5%	97.1%

Task 7.2

Organisation	Possible productivity measures
Taxi firm	– number of fares per shift – number of miles per shift
Hospital	– out-patients seen per day
Motorbike courier service	– miles per week – number of packages per day
Firm of accountants	– chargeable hours as a percentage of total hours
Retail store	– sales per employee – sales per square foot of shop floor
Maker of hand-made pottery	– number of pots thrown per day – number of pots painted per day

Task 7.3

The total value added is £394,200

The value added per employee is £26,280

Workings

	£
Sales	1,447,600
Less: cost of materials	(736,500)
cost of services	(316,900)
Total value added	394,200
Value added per employee	£394,200/15
	£26,280

Task 7.4

	January	February	March
Productivity per labour hour	0.99 units	1.11 units	1.00 units
Efficiency ratio	108.8%	122.0%	110.5%
Capacity ratio	92.4%	86.7%	88.8%
Activity ratio	100.5%	105.7%	98.1%
Value added per employee	£6,613	£6,445	£5,784

Workings

(a)

		January	February	March
(i)	Productivity per labour hour	$\dfrac{8,540}{8,635}$	$\dfrac{8,670}{7,820}$	$\dfrac{9,320}{9,280}$
		0.99 units per hour	1.11 units per hour	1.00 unit per hour
(ii)	Efficiency ratio	$\dfrac{8,540 \times 1.1}{8,635}$	$\dfrac{8,670 \times 1.1}{7,820}$	$\dfrac{9,320 \times 1.1}{9,280}$
		108.8%	122.0%	110.5%
(iii)	Capacity ratio	$\dfrac{8,635}{8,500 \times 1.1}$	$\dfrac{7,820}{8,200 \times 1.1}$	$\dfrac{9,280}{9,500 \times 1.1}$
		92.4%	86.7%	88.8%
(iv)	Activity ratio	$\dfrac{8,540}{8,500}$	$\dfrac{8,670}{8,200}$	$\dfrac{9,320}{9,500}$
		100.5%	105.7%	98.1%

(v)	Value added per employee	£	£	£
	Sales	916,000	923,000	965,000
	Production costs	(552,300)	(568,500)	(629,500)
	Value added	363,700	354,500	335,500
	Value added per employee	£6,613	£6,445	£5,784

(b) Both the productivity per hour and efficiency indicators show that in all three months the time taken to produce units is less than the standard time of 1.1 hours. Although the activity ratio shows that in all three months the actual activity level was fairly close to the budgeted level, the capacity ratio indicates that the available hours of work were never exceeded. Production significantly increased in March but this appears to have caused a lower value added per employee.

Task 7.5

	Calculation	Explanation
Efficiency ratio	92.61%	As the efficiency ratio is less than 100% this indicates that the workforce have not worked as efficiently as was anticipated. The actual hours worked are more than the standard hours for that level of production.
Capacity ratio	102.22%	The capacity ratio indicates whether as many hours have been worked as were budgeted for. In this instance the capacity ratio is greater than 100% meaning that the number of hours worked was more than those budgeted for.
Production volume ratio	94.67%	The production volume ratio is an indicator of how the volume of actual production compares to the budgeted level of output. In this instance as the production volume ratio is below 100% this indicates that the actual level of output was below the budgeted level.

Workings

(a) Efficiency ratio $= \dfrac{\text{Standard hours for actual production}}{\text{Actual hours worked}} \times 100$

$= \dfrac{14,200 \times 3}{46,000} \times 100$

$= 92.61\%$

Capacity ratio $= \dfrac{\text{Actual hours worked}}{\text{Budgeted hours}} \times 100$

$= \dfrac{46,000}{15,000 \times 3} \times 100$

$= 102.22\%$

Production volume ratio $= \dfrac{\text{Actual output}}{\text{Budgeted output}} \times 100$

$= \dfrac{14,200}{15,000} \times 100$

$= 94.67\%$

(b) Hours worked @ 95% efficiency $= \dfrac{14,200 \times 3}{0.95}$

$$= \quad 44,842$$

Hours saved $(46,000 - 44,842) \quad = \quad 1{,}158$ hours

Task 7.6

Gross profit margin	38%
Operating profit margin	12.7%
Return on capital employed	14.4%
Asset turnover	1.13
Non-current (fixed) asset turnover	1.38
Current ratio	3.19 : 1
Quick ratio	2.19 : 1
Receivables' (debtors') collection period	55 days
Inventory (stock) turnover period in days	41 days
Payables' (creditors') payment period	42 days
Interest cover	9.35 times
Gearing ratio	34.5%

Workings

(a) (i) Gross profit margin

$$= \frac{\text{Gross profit}}{\text{Revenue (turnover)}} \times 100$$

$$= \frac{1,007,200}{2,650,400} \times 100$$

$$= 38\%$$

(ii) Operating profit margin

$$= \frac{\text{Operating profit}}{\text{Revenue}} \times 100$$

$$= \frac{336,600}{2,650,400} \times 100$$

$$= 12.7\%$$

(iii) Return on capital employed $=$

$$\frac{\text{Operating profit}}{\text{'Non-current (fixed) assets + net current assets'}} \times 100$$

$$= \frac{336,600}{2,337,500} \times 100$$

$$= 14.4\%$$

(iv) Asset turnover $= \dfrac{\text{Revenue}}{\text{Capital employed}}$

$= \dfrac{2{,}650{,}400}{2{,}337{,}500}$

$= 1.13$

(v) Non-current asset turnover $= \dfrac{\text{Revenue}}{\text{Non} - \text{current assets}}$

$= \dfrac{2{,}650{,}400}{1{,}920{,}400}$

$= 1.38$

(vi) Current ratio $= \dfrac{\text{Current assets}}{\text{Current liabilities}}$

$= \dfrac{607{,}400}{190{,}300}$

$= 3.19 : 1$

(vii) Quick ratio $= \dfrac{\text{Current assets} - \text{inventory}}{\text{Current liabilities}}$

$= \dfrac{607{,}400 - 191{,}200}{190{,}300}$

$= 2.19 : 1$

(viii) Receivables' collection period $= \dfrac{\text{Receivables}}{\text{Revenue}} \times 365$

$= \dfrac{399{,}400}{2{,}650{,}400} \times 365$

$= 55 \text{ days}$

(ix) Inventory days $= \dfrac{\text{Average inventory}}{\text{Cost of sales}} \times 365$

$= \dfrac{(180{,}000 + 191{,}200)/2}{1{,}643{,}200} \times 365$

$= 41 \text{ days}$

(x) Payables' payment period $= \dfrac{\text{Payables}}{\text{Purchases}} \times 365$

$= \dfrac{190{,}300}{1{,}654{,}400} \times 365$

$= 42 \text{ days}$

(xi) Interest cover

$$= \frac{\text{Profit before interest}}{\text{Interest charge}}$$

$$= \frac{336,600}{36,000}$$

$$= 9.35$$

(xii) Gearing ratio

$$= \frac{\text{Long term loans}}{\text{Share capital + reserves}}$$

$$= \frac{600,000}{1,737,500}$$

$$= 34.5\%$$

(b) Increase in cash balance

$$= \frac{£1,654,400}{365} \times (60 - 42)$$

$$= £81,587$$

．．．

Task 7.7

(a)

	July	Aug	Sept	Oct	Nov	Dec
Gross profit margin	34%	34%	34%	32%	31%	31%
Operating profit margin	12%	12%	12%	11%	10%	9%
Expenses to sales %	22%	22%	22%	21%	21%	22%
Return on capital employed (W1)	15.2%	14.6%	13.1%	11.6%	10.9%	10.0%
Asset turnover (W2)	1.27	1.21	1.09	1.06	1.09	1.11

(b) Sales revenue decreased from July to September and then increased significantly until the end of the year. However the increase in sales has been at the cost of the gross profit margin which has decreased from 34% to 31%. Although the expenses to sales percentage has remained reasonably constant over the period, the operating profit margin has fallen due to the decrease in gross profit margin.

Return on capital employed fell dramatically in the first four months of the period although this was due to a significant decrease in asset turnover in that period more than a decline in profitability. The fall in return on capital employed continues in the last three months of the year due to the fall in operating profit margin; however the drop in return is not as bad as it might have been, as the asset turnover is again improving.

Workings

1. Here, return on capital employed is calculated as

$$\text{ROCE} = \frac{\text{Profit before interest}}{\text{Capital employed}} = \frac{(550 - 374 - 116)}{468 + 50} = 11.6\% \text{ for October, etc}$$
$$\text{(shareholders funds + loan)}$$

Alternatively, it may be computed as a return on equity:

$$\text{ROCE (RoE)} = \frac{\text{Profit after interest}}{\text{Shareholders' funds}} = \frac{(550-374-116-3)}{468} = 12.2\% \text{ for October, etc}$$

2. To be consistent with the ROCE definition used, asset turnover has been calculated as

$$\text{Asset turnover} = \frac{\text{Revenue (turnover)}}{\text{Total capital employed}} = \frac{550}{468+50} = 1.06 \text{ for October, etc}$$
$$\text{(shareholders' funds + loan)}$$

Task 7.8

(a)

	20X6	20X7	20X8
Gross profit margin	40.1%	39.1%	37.9%
Operating profit margin	14.1%	13.0%	11.0%
Return on capital employed	13.3%	11.9%	10.6%
(Note: total CE used ie share capital and reserves + long term loan)			
Asset turnover	0.95	0.92	0.97
Non-current (fixed) asset turnover	1.29	1.20	1.16
Current ratio	3.9 : 1	3.5 : 1	2.6 : 1
Quick ratio	3.1 : 1	2.6 : 1	1.6 : 1
Receivables' (debtors') collection period	40 days	46 days	48 days
Inventory (stock) turnover in days	45 days	54 days	64 days
Payables' (creditors') payment period	60 days	62 days	65 days

(b) Profitability has fallen significantly over the three-year period. Return on capital employed has fallen by almost 3% points and this is due solely to decreases in gross and operating profit margins, as asset turnover has remained fairly constant with a minor increase in 20X8. Although both gross profit margin and operating profit margin have fallen, the operating profit margin has fallen proportionally a great deal more.

This means that as well as the gross profit margin falling, the expenses of the business are increasing.

There also seems to have been some loss of control regarding the working capital of the business. The inventory turnover period has increased dramatically, meaning that large amounts of funds are being tied up in inventory holding. Receivables' days have also increased by eight days whereas the payables' payment period has only increased by five days over the three-year period.

The overall working capital of the business does appear to be high, particularly the high cash balances at the end of 20X6 and 20X7. This has improved by 20X8 but this may be as a result of the inventory turnover increase rather than a conscious policy.

Workings

	20X6	20X7	20X8
	£000	£000	£000
Income statement (Profit and loss account) summary			
Revenue (turnover)	1,420	1,560	1,740
Cost of sales	(850)	(950)	(1,080)
Gross profit	570	610	660
Expenses	(370)	(407)	(469)
Operating profit	200	203	191
Interest	–	(7)	(6)
Profit after interest	200	196	185
Statement of financial position (Balance sheet) summary			
Non-current assets	1,100	1,300	1,500
Inventory	105	140	190
Receivables	155	198	230
Cash	280	224	73
Payables	(140)	(162)	(193)
	1,500	1,700	1,800
Long term loan	–	(100)	(100)
Share capital and reserves	1,500	1,600	1,700

	20X6	20X7	20X8
Gross profit margin	570/1,420	610/1,560	660/1,740
Operating profit margin	200/1,420	203/1,560	191/1,740
Return on capital employed	200/1,500	203/1,700	191/1,800
(Note: total CE used i.e. share capital & reserves + long term loan)			
Asset turnover	1,420/1,500	1,560/1,700	1,740/1,800
Non-current asset turnover	1,420/1,100	1,560/1,300	1,740/1,500
Current ratio	540/140	562/162	493/193
Quick ratio	435/140	422/162	303/193
Receivables' collection period	155/1,420 × 365	198/1,560 × 365	230/1,740 × 365
Inventory turnover in days	105/850 × 365	140/950 × 365	190/1,080 × 365
Payables' payment period	140/850 × 365	162/950 × 365	193/1,080 × 365

....

Task 7.9

(a)

	North	South	Central
Gross profit margin	32.0%	30.0%	35.0%
Operating profit margin	18.0%	11.1%	13.4%
Return on capital employed	16.0%	9.0%	14.0%
Asset turnover	0.89	0.81	1.04
Inventory (stock) turnover in months	0.7 months	1.1 months	1.0 months
Receivables' (debtors') collection period in months	1.4 months	2.3 months	1.6 months
Payables' (creditors') payment period in months	2.1 months	1.3 months	1.9 months
Units per square metre	34.0 units	25.5 units	29.3 units
Units per employee	944 units	850 units	820 units
Units per hour	2 units	1.8 units	1.8 units

(b)   In terms of profitability North is clearly the most profitable with the highest operating profit margin and return on capital employed. However Central has a higher gross profit margin which may be due to production of a different product to North or due to higher local selling prices or lower purchasing prices for Central. Although Central's operating profit margin is significantly lower than North's its return on capital employed is not so different due to a higher asset turnover in Central. South seems to have profitability problems with gross and operating profit margins, asset turnover and return on capital employed significantly lower than those of the other two divisions.

North again appears to have the best working capital control with the lowest inventory turnover and receivables' collection period and the longest payables' payment period. Central's working capital control appears to be adequate but again there are questions to be asked at South with a relatively long receivables' collection period and a month shorter payables' payment period.

Finally, whichever way productivity is measured, the productivity at North is significantly greater than at either of the other two divisions. Central makes the same number of units per hour as South but less per employee, indicating that there could be room for improvement in employee productivity at Central.

Workings

	North £	South £	Central £
Income statement (Profit and loss account)			
Revenue	870,000	560,000	640,000
COS: Opening inventory	34,000	41,000	34,000
Purchases	590,000	380,000	420,000
Closing inventory	(32,000)	(29,000)	(38,000)
	592,000	392,000	416,000
Gross profit	278,000	168,000	224,000
Expenses	(121,000)	(106,000)	(138,000)
Operating profit	157,000	62,000	86,000
Statement of financial position (Balance sheet)			
Receivables	100,100	107,300	87,600
Payables	(103,400)	(42,600)	(66,700)
Other net assets	983,300	625,300	594,100
Capital	980,000	690,000	615,000

	North	South	Central
Gross profit margin	278/870	168/560	224/640
Operating profit margin	157/870	62/560	86/640
Return on capital employed	157/980	62/690	86/615
Asset turnover	870/980	560/690	640/615
Inventory turnover in months (using average inventory)	33/592 x 12	35/392 x 12	36/416 x 12
Receivables' collection period in months	100.1/870 x 12	107.3/560 x 12	87.6/640 x 12
Payables' payment period in months	103.4/592 x 12	42.6/392 x 12	66.7/416 x 12
Units per square metre	17,000/500	10,200/400	12,300/420
Units per employee	17,000/18	10,200/12	12,300/15
Units per hour	17,000/8,500	10,200/5,800	12,300/7,000

Task 7.10

(i)	Gross profit	=	380,000 x 0.48
		=	£182,400
(ii)	Sales	=	£425,000/0.34
		=	£1,250,000
(iii)	Gross profit	=	£85,000 x 0.40
		=	£34,000
	Operating profit	=	£85,000 x 0.115
		=	£9,775
	Expenses	=	£34,000 – £9,775
		=	£24,225
(iv)	Capital employed	=	£100,000/0.116
		=	£862,069
(v)	Asset turnover	=	0.10/0.08
		=	1.25
(vi)	Average inventory (stock)	=	(£158,000 + £182,000)/2
		=	£170,000
	Cost of sales	=	£158,000 + £560,000 – £182,000
		=	£536,000
	Inventory turnover	=	£536,000/£170,000
		=	3.2 times
(vii)	Sales	=	£96,000/48 x 365
		=	£730,000

Task 7.11

(a)

	Y/e 31 Dec 20X8	Y/e 31 Dec 20X7
Gross profit margin	45.3%	42.4%
Operating profit margin (Operating profit/revenue (turnover))	18.3%	17.0%
Return on capital employed (Operating profit/ share capital + retained earnings + loan)	14.7%	13.9%
Asset turnover	0.80	0.82
Non-current (fixed) asset turnover	0.85	0.89
Current ratio	1.75 : 1	2.3 : 1
Quick ratio	1.2 : 1	1.6 : 1
Receivables' (debtors') collection period	40 days	44 days
Inventory (stock)Inventory turnover	31 days	36 days
Payables' (creditors') payment period	61 days	51 days
Interest cover	11.0	9.6
Gearing ratio (loans/share capital + retained earnings)	25%	27.8%

(b) Return on capital employed has increased over the two-year period and this is solely due to increased profitability as both the asset turnover and non-current asset turnover have decreased over the period. There has been a significant increase in gross profit margin in 20X8 and, although operating profit margin has also increased, it has not done so at the rate of the gross profit margin, indicating that expenses are in fact increasing at a faster rate than sales. This may be due to a large advertising campaign which has increased costs but allowed the gross profit margin to increase or some similar reason.

As well as an increase in sales and profitability there also appears to be general improvement in the working capital management. Both the current and quick ratios have fallen but are still at acceptable levels. The receivables' collection period and inventory turnover period have both been reduced by a few days and in combination with the increase in the payables' payment period by 10 days this will have a significant positive effect on the cash flows of the business.

The level of gearing does not appear to be a problem, as the gearing ratios are quite low and the interest cover is quite high.

Task 7.12

(a) To: Angela Wade

From: A Technician

Date: xx.xx.xx

Subject: **West Ltd and East Ltd – Performance Report**

(i) **Return on capital employed (ROCE)**

The ROCE is a key financial ratio which shows the amount of profit which has been made in relation to the amount of resources invested. It also gives some idea of how efficiently the company has been operating.

$$ROCE = \frac{\text{Operating profit}}{\text{Net assets}}$$

$$\text{ROCE (West Ltd)} = \frac{3,068}{15,340} = 0.2 \times 100\% = 20\%$$

$$\text{ROCE (East Ltd)} = \frac{2,795}{6,500} = 0.43 \times 100\% = 43\%$$

(ii) **Asset turnover**

The asset turnover is one of the main ratios for the statement of financial position (balance sheet), and is a measure of how well the assets of a business are being used to generate sales.

$$\text{Asset turnover} = \frac{\text{Net revenue (turnover)}}{\text{Net assets}}$$

$$\text{Asset turnover (West Ltd)} = \frac{17,910}{15,340} = 1.17 \text{ times}$$

$$\text{Asset turnover (East Ltd)} = \frac{17,424}{6,500} = 2.68 \text{ times}$$

(iii) **Sales margin**

The sales margin ratio is a measure of overall profitability and it provides a measure of performance for management. Unsatisfactory sales margins are investigated by management, and are generally followed by control action. Increasing selling prices and reducing costs will have a direct effect on this ratio.

$$\text{Sales margin} = \frac{\text{Operating profit}}{\text{Net revenue'}}$$

$$\text{Sales margin (West Ltd)} = \frac{3,068}{17,910} = 0.171 \times 100\% = 17.1\%$$

$$\text{Sales margin (East Ltd)} = \frac{2,795}{17,424} = 0.16 \times 100\% = 16\%$$

(b) **Measure of customer service: faulty sales**

The percentage of faulty sales as a measure of the level of customer service is calculated as:

$$\frac{\text{Returns}}{\text{Gross sales}}$$

West Ltd$=\dfrac{100}{20,000}=0.005\% \times 100\%=0.5\%$

East Ltd$=\dfrac{220}{22,000}=0.01\% \times 100\%=1\%$

(c) **Further measure of customer service**

Another possible measure of the level of customer service which could be derived from the accounting data is the number of days between order and delivery of goods.

This can be calculated as follows.

$$\text{Time between order and delivery}=\frac{\text{Orders received in year-net sales ('000 litres)}}{\text{Net sales ('000 litres)}} \times 365 \text{ days}$$

West Ltd$=\dfrac{20,173-19,900}{19,900} \times 365 \text{ days} = 5 \text{ days}$

East Ltd$=\dfrac{22,854-21,780}{21,780} \times 365 \text{ days} = 18 \text{ days}$

The amount of money which the subsidiaries invest in research and development, and training could also provide a measure of customer service.

(d) **Limitations of financial ratios**

Financial ratios as a measure of performance are only concerned with the data recorded in the accounts. For example, East Ltd appears to be a much more efficient company than West Ltd based on its ROCE and asset turnover ratios. However, when calculations are made to measure customer service, West Ltd has far fewer days between order and delivery of goods, and half as many faulty sales (as a percentage of gross sales).

The financial ratios also treat research and development, and training costs as expenses which are written off to the income statement (profit and loss account). These expenses are likely to have an impact on the future profitability of the company, and are more of an investment than expense.

Both West Ltd and East Ltd use plant of similar size and technology. There is however, a large difference in the net book values of the plant, and hence a large difference in the net assets of each company.

East Ltd purchased its plant before West Ltd, and has a lower cost, and a higher depreciation to date than West Ltd. These differences arise mainly due to the fact that the accounts are prepared using historic cost accounting. The fact that East Ltd's net assets are so much lower than those of West Ltd, means that the ROCE of East Ltd will be much higher than that of West Ltd.

Task 7.13

(a)

Performance indicator	Workings	
Return on capital employed	(operating profit ÷ net assets) × 100% (975,000/4,875,000) × 100%	20%
Asset turnover	revenue/net assets 3,900,000/4,875,000	0.8
Sales (or operating profit) margin	(operating profit/revenue (turnover)) × 100% (975,000/3,900,000) × 100%	25%
Average age of receivables (debtors) in months	(receivables/revenue) × 12 (325,000/3,900,000) × 12	1 month
Average age of finished inventory (stock) in months	(average finished goods inventory /cost of sales) × 12 (½ x (140,000 + 50,000)/840,000) × 12	1.4 months

(b) **Briefing notes on the usefulness of performance indicators**

Prepared for Angela Frear

Prepared by Financial Analyst

Dated: xx.xx.xx

(i) **Return on capital employed**

The return on capital employed can be misleading.

(1) Profits should be related to average capital employed but we compute the ratio using year-end assets. Using year-end figures can distort trends and comparisons. If a new investment is undertaken near to a year end and financed, for example, by an issue of shares, the capital employed will rise by the finance raised but profits will only have a month or two of the new investment's contribution.

(2) The ROCE would be higher if costs such as marketing, research and development and training were not treated as revenue expenditure but were viewed as investment for the future and were capitalised.

(ii) **Sales (operating profit) margin**

The sales (or operating profit) margin can be manipulated in a number of ways. The following activities would result in short-term improvements in the margin, but probably at the expense of the organisation's long-term viability:

(1) Reducing expenditure on discretionary cost items such as research and development

(2) Depreciating assets over a longer period of time, so that the depreciation charge is less

(3) Choosing an alternative inventory valuation method to increase the value of closing inventory

(iii) **Average delay in fulfilling orders**

	£
Orders during the year	4,550,000
Revenue during the year	3,900,000
Unfulfilled orders	650,000

Average delay = (£650,000/£3,900,000) × 12 months = 2 months

(iv) **Measures of customer satisfaction**

As well as the delay in fulfilling orders, other measures of customer satisfaction include the following.

- Repeat business ((£3,120,000/£3,900,000) × 100% = 80%)

- Cost of customer support per £ of revenue (£400,000/£3,900,000 = 10p)

- Cost of customer support per customer (information not available)

(v) **Measuring performance from an internal perspective**

A number of indicators may help to measure performance from an internal perspective.

- Training costs as a percentage of production costs ((£140,000/£930,000) × 100% = 15.05%)

- Reworked faulty production as a percentage of total production ((£37,200/£930,000) × 100% = 4%)

- Returns as a percentage of sales ((£100,000/£4m) × 100% = 2.5%)

The first indicator should be relatively high, the second and third as low as possible.

(vi) **Measuring the innovation and learning perspective**

The innovation and learning perspective could be measured with one of the following indicators.

- Revenue from new products as a percentage of total revenue ((£1.56m/£3.9m) × 100% = 40%)

- Research and development expenditure as a percentage of cost of production ((£750,000/£930,000) × 100% = 81%)

- Research and development expenditure as a percentage of revenue ((£750,000/£3.9m) × 100% = 19.2%)

Note: A fuller answer has been given here than was required in the task for assessment purposes, where in most cases only ONE point was required.

Task 7.14

(a) (i) Gross profit margin $= \dfrac{£221,760}{£633,600} \times 100\% = 35\%$

    (ii) Operating profit margin $= \dfrac{£76,032}{£633,600} \times 100\% = 12\%$

    (iii) Return on capital employed $= \dfrac{£76,032}{£95,040} \times 100\% = 80\%$

    (iv) Asset turnover $= \dfrac{£633,600}{£95,040} = 6.7$ times

    (v) No. of passengers in the year $= \dfrac{\text{revenue (turnover)}}{\text{fare per passenger}} = \dfrac{£633,600}{£1}$

        $= 633,600$ passengers

    (vi) Total cost per mile $= \dfrac{£633,600 - £76,032}{356,400} = £1.56$

    (vii) No. of journeys in the year $= \dfrac{356,400 \text{ miles}}{18 \text{ miles per journey}} = 19,800$ journeys

        No. of journeys per day $= \dfrac{19,800}{360} = 55$ journeys

    (viii) Maintenance cost per mile $= \dfrac{£28,512}{356,400} = £0.08$

    (ix) Passengers per day $= \dfrac{633,600 \text{ (from v))}}{360} = 1,760$ passengers

    (x) Passengers per journey $= \dfrac{1,760 \text{ (from(ix))}}{55 \text{ (from(vii))}} = 32$ passengers

    (xi) Number of drivers $= \dfrac{\text{wages paid}}{\text{wages per driver}} = \dfrac{£142,000}{£14,200}$

        $= 10$ drivers

(b) **MEMO**

To: Chief executive

From: Management accountant

Date: xx.xx.xx

Subject: **Performance of Travel Bus Ltd for the year to 30 November 20X8**

This memo addresses a number of issues concerning the productivity and profitability of Travel Bus Ltd.

(i) **Productivity and profitability**

Productivity is the quantity of service produced (output) in relation to the resources put in (input). It measures how efficiently resources are being used.

An increase in productivity does not always lead to increased profitability. For example the number of passengers carried per driver, a measure of productivity, could increase. The extra passengers may have been attracted by offering substantial fare reductions, however, and this could lead to reduced profitability.

Another example might be an increase in productivity in terms of the number of journeys per bus. This increase in 'output' arising from the increase in productivity may not be saleable: the buses may be running empty. The revenue gained might be less than the additional costs incurred, leading to reduced profitability.

(ii) **Driver productivity**

A possible measure of driver productivity is the number of miles per driver.

	20X7	20X8
Miles per driver	$\dfrac{324,000}{8} = 40,500$	$\dfrac{356,400}{10} = 35,640$

The number of miles per driver has decreased between 20X7 and 20X8 and so, in terms of this measure of productivity, the drivers' claim that their productivity has increased is incorrect.

Even if the productivity had increased, the drivers might still be unable to claim that this had resulted in improved profitability. As discussed above, the extra miles might have been travelled with too few fare-paying passengers, so profitability would not necessarily have improved.

(iii) **Reason for improved profitability**

A major reason for the improved profitability was the Council's decision not to charge for parking. This reduced the overall cost of using the service for passengers, and demand therefore increased considerably. Since many of the costs incurred by Travel Bus Ltd are fixed, costs did not increase at the same rate as revenue (turnover), and profitability improved.

(iv) **Performance indicators to measure the satisfaction of passenger needs**

(1) The satisfaction of passenger needs could be monitored by the number of passengers per journey.

	20X7	20X8
Number of passengers per journey	30	32

Depending on the size of the buses, passenger needs may have been less satisfied during 20X8 because of more crowding or the need to stand because no seats were available.

Another measure of the satisfaction of passenger needs is the number of journeys per day.

	20X7	20X8
Number of journeys per day	50	55

This increase probably led to reduced waiting times and so passenger needs may have been better satisfied in 20X8.

(2) A measure of the satisfaction of customer needs that cannot be derived from the existing data is cleanliness of the buses.

Monitoring the cleaning cost per day or per bus might give some indication of the effort put into keeping the buses clean.

Another measure of the satisfaction of customer needs is punctuality of the buses and their adherence to published timetables.

Monitoring the percentage of buses arriving and departing within five minutes of their published time would give an indication of performance in this area.

Note. Only one measure required by the task

(v) **Monitoring the safety aspect of Travel Bus's operations**

(1) The safety aspect of Travel Bus's operations could be monitored by the maintenance cost per mile.

	20X7	20X8
Maintenance cost per mile	£0.10	£0.08

This has reduced, which may indicate a reduction in attention to safety, especially as maintenance costs are likely to increase as buses become older. No new buses have been added to the fleet (cost value of buses has remained at £240,000); the buses are older and likely to require more maintenance.

On the other hand, some of this reduction in the cost per mile may have been caused by the spreading of the fixed element of maintenance costs over a higher number of miles in the year 20X8.

Another indicator of attention to the safety aspect might be the average age of the buses. The depreciation charge for the year 20X8 was £12,000 (£180,000 – £168,000). On a cost value of £240,000, assuming straight line depreciation and no residual value, this suggests a useful life of 20 years. Accumulated depreciation of £180,000 means that the buses were on average 15 years old by the end of 20X6, and thus nearing the end of their useful lives.

(2) A measure of the safety aspect that cannot be derived from the existing data is the number of accidents per year.

Another measure could be the percentage of maintenance cost that is incurred to prevent faults compared with the percentage incurred to correct faults. This would indicate whether faults were being prevented before they occurred, or whether maintenance was being carried out 'after the event', which could compromise safety.

Note. Only one measure required by the task.

Task 7.15

(a) **Budgeted income statements (profit and loss accounts)**

	Pickmaster	Pickmaster 2
	£	£
Revenue (turnover)	1,125,000	1,125,000
Cost of sales		
Tea pickers	150,000	150,000
Tea processor operators (W)	48,000	4,800
Depreciation (W)	16,000	72,000
Seed and fertiliser costs	75,000	75,000
Total cost of sales	289,000	301,800
Gross profit	836,000	823,200
Administration costs	150,000	135,000
Distribution costs	350,000	350,000
Operating profit	336,000	338,200

Net assets at year end

	Pickmaster	Pickmaster 2
	£	£
Budgeted net assets	935,500	935,500
Operating profit	336,000	338,200
	1,271,500	1,273,700

Workings

	Pickmaster	Pickmaster 2
	£	£
Tea processor operators (10 × £6 × 100 × 8)	48,000	
(1 × £6 × 100 × 8)		4,800
Depreciation of tea machines (8 × £2,000)	16,000	
(8 × £9,000)		72,000

Tutorial note. The value of the new machines has not been included in the net asset figure as their purchase would have to be funded in some way ie bank loan, leasing, leading to an increase in liabilities which would cancel out the increase in asset values. This will not be an exact cancellation but we have no information about the method of funding.

(b)

	Pickmaster	Pickmaster 2
Gross profit margin	74.31%	73.17%
Operating profit margin	29.87%	30.06%
Return on net assets	26.43%	26.55%

Workings

		Pickmaster	Pickmaster 2
		%	%
(i)	**Gross profit margin**		
	$\dfrac{836,000}{1,125,000} \times 100$	74.31	
	$\dfrac{823,200}{1,125,000} \times 100$		73.17
(ii)	**Operating profit margin**		
	$\dfrac{336,000}{1,125,000} \times 100$	29.87	
	$\dfrac{338,200}{1,125,000} \times 100$		30.06

	Pickmaster	Pickmaster 2
(iii) **Return on net assets**		
$\dfrac{336,000}{1,271,500} \times 100$	26.43	
$\dfrac{338,200}{1,273,700} \times 100$		26.55

(c)

REPORT

To: Managing Director

From: Accounting technician

Date: December 20X7

Subject: Purchase of new machinery

I have been asked to write this report with regard to the decision as to whether to replace our current tea machines with eight new Pickmaster machines or Pickmaster 2 machines.

Performance indicators

(i)   In terms of our profitability and return on net assets, there is little to be chosen between the two options. The Pickmaster machines give a slightly higher gross profit margin due to the much smaller depreciation charge, although costing more in terms of tea processor operators. However due to a reduction in administration costs if the Pickmaster 2 machines are purchased, then the gross profit and operating profit margins hardly differ under the two options. Equally the return on net assets under each of the two options is very similar.

Other considerations

(ii) Firstly we need to consider the funding of the purchase of these machines. If the Pickmaster machines are purchased then they will cost £160,000 (8 x £20,000) but if the Pickmaster 2 machines are purchased then these will cost £720,000 (8 x £90,000). These purchases will have to be funded in some way such as a bank loan or by purchasing them under lease finance. In either event if the Pickmaster 2 machines are purchased then this will significantly increase the gearing of the organisation and incur high service costs in the form of interest payments on a loan or finance charges on a lease.

The second consideration is the relative benefits and costs of the two machines. The advantage of the Pickmaster 2 is that only 1 operator per day is required rather than 10. However these operators are employed as and when needed on temporary contracts, therefore if the harvest was low less operatives could be employed. However the depreciation charges on the machines at £72,000 (8 x £9,000) for the Pickmaster 2 machines compared to £16,000 (8 x £2,000) for the Pickmaster machines are fixed costs that will be incurred whatever the level of revenue (turnover) and harvest. Therefore if there is a low harvest investment in the Pickmaster 2 machines will depress profit.

(**Tutorial note.** A third consideration might be the expected residual value of each type of machine at the end of the 10-year period but only two further considerations were required for the task).

Conclusion

(iii) As the choice of machines has little effect on profit at the budgeted level but the Pickmaster 2 machines increase the risk of the operation, due to increased gearing and depreciation charges, then on balance purchase of the Pickmaster machines for £160,000 would be recommended.

....

Task 7.16

(a) **Performance indicators**

	September	October	November

Profit margin

$$\frac{£148,687}{£690,000} \times 100 \qquad \frac{£154,125}{£697,200} \times 100 \qquad \frac{£125,480}{£672,000} \times 100$$

$$= 21.55\% \qquad\qquad = 22.11\% \qquad\qquad = 18.67\%$$

Direct material cost as a percentage of revenue (turnover)

$$\frac{£185,000}{£690,000} \times 100 \qquad \frac{£185,100}{£697,200} \times 100 \qquad \frac{£185,220}{£672,000} \times 100$$

$$= 26.81\% \qquad\qquad = 26.55\% \qquad\qquad = 27.56\%$$

Direct labour cost as a percentage of revenue

$$\frac{£274,313}{£690,000} \times 100 \qquad \frac{£275,975}{£697,200} \times 100 \qquad \frac{£279,300}{£672,000} \times 100$$

$$= 39.76\% \qquad\qquad = 39.58\% \qquad\qquad = 41.56\%$$

Return on capital employed (ROCE)

$$\frac{£148,687}{£1,211,000} \times 100 \qquad \frac{£154,125}{£1,218,700} \times 100 \qquad \frac{£125,480}{£1,204,700} \times 100$$

$$= 12.28\% \qquad\qquad = 12.65\% \qquad\qquad = 10.42\%$$

Alternatively:

$$\frac{£148,687}{£2,011,000} \times 100 \qquad \frac{£154,125}{£2,018,700} \times 100 \qquad \frac{£125,480}{£2,004,700} \times 100$$

$$= 7.39\% \qquad\qquad = 7.63\% \qquad\qquad = 6.26\%$$

Meals produced as a percentage of orders

$$\frac{115,500}{115,000} \qquad\qquad \frac{116,200}{117,000} \qquad\qquad \frac{117,600}{112,000}$$

$$= 100.43\% \qquad\qquad = 99.32\% \qquad\qquad = 105.00\%$$

Meals produced as a percentage of capacity

$$\frac{115,500}{125,000} \qquad\qquad \frac{116,200}{125,000} \qquad\qquad \frac{117,600}{125,000}$$

$$= 92.4\% \qquad\qquad = 92.96\% \qquad\qquad = 94.08\%$$

(b)

REPORT

To:	Managing Director
From:	Accounting Technician
Subject:	Performance of the Catering Division
Date:	7 December 20X6

This report examines key areas of the performance of the catering division in November 20X6.

1. Overall, the division performed significantly worse in November compared with the previous two months. Profit margin fell by 13% from 21.55% in October to 18.67%, and ROCE fell by 15% from 12.28% to 10.42% in the same period.

2   The problem in the division arises from the difference between meals ordered and meals produced in November. 117,600 meals were produced, which was 5% greater than the number ordered of 112,000. As the meals are perishable, excess production one day cannot be used the next day, and so leads to wastage.

3   The excess production in November meant that materials and labour costs were increased without the costs being recovered in increased sales.

4   The division worked at 94.08% of capacity in the month. We would not expect full capacity at all times as work should only be done to fulfil orders placed.

(c)

	Renting	Purchasing
(i)	£	£
Revenue (120,000 × £6)	720,000	720,000
Cost of sales		
Materials (120,000 × £2)	240,000	240,000
Labour (120,000 × £1.50)	180,000	180,000
Fixed overheads	82,000	82,000
Rent	50,000	
Depreciation (£3m – £900,000)/(12 × 10 months)		17,500
Total cost of sales	552,000	519,500
Profit	168,000	200,500
Net assets		
(£1,204,700 + £168,000)	1,372,700	
(£1,204,700 + £1m + £200,500)		2,405,200

(ii)

	Renting	Purchasing
Profit margin =	$\dfrac{£168,000}{£720,000} \times 100$	$\dfrac{£200,500}{£720,000} \times 100$
	= 23.33%	= 27.85%
ROCE =	$\dfrac{£168,000}{£1,372,700} \times 100$	$\dfrac{£200,500}{£2,405,200} \times 100$
	= 12.24%	= 8.34%

(iii) Renting the machine gives a higher ROCE than buying the machine because the higher profit earned with a bought machine is outweighed by the large increase in net assets. Therefore the machine should be rented rather than bought. However, the ROCE is not necessarily improved when compared with the figures for October to November 20X6, and further consideration should be given to whether the machine is obtained at all.

Chapter 8

Task 8.1

		Type of cost
(i)	lost contribution on defective products sold as seconds	Internal failure
(ii)	cost of replacing faulty products	External failure
(iii)	claims from customers relating to defective products	External failure
(iv)	products scrapped due to faulty raw materials	Internal failure
(v)	training for quality control staff	Prevention
(vi)	maintenance of quality control equipment	Prevention
(vii)	performance testing of finished goods	Appraisal
(viii)	costs of customer after sales service department	External failure
(ix)	costs of inspection of raw materials	Appraisal
(x)	costs of production delays due to re-working defective products discovered in quality inspection	Internal failure

Task 8.2

		Prevention	Appraisal	Internal failure	External failure
(i)	Zippers	Increase due to costs of design	No effect	Reduced as product is more reliable	Reduced as zipper has longer lifespan
(ii)	Jumpers	No effect	Increase as machines need to be checked regularly	Increase due to investigation, repairs to machines and re-inspection costs	Damages claims from customers and loss of future sales.
(iii)	Men's suits	Finding a new supplier	Increase due to inspection procedures	Lost contribution but reduction of costs as benefits from inspection controls are felt	Reduce as fewer defective products sold

Task 8.3

Explicit costs of quality

- costs of repairing defective products

- costs of quality control inspections

- costs of repair of returned goods from customers

Implicit costs of quality

- the opportunity cost of lost sales to customers who are dissatisfied due to faulty goods and will not purchase from the organisation again

- loss of goodwill or reputation due to factors such as the widespread recall of one of an organisation's products

- costs of production disruption due to reworking of faulty products – these costs will be included in the production costs but cannot be separately identified

• •

Task 8.4

Prevention costs	None
Appraisal costs	£35,000
Internal failure costs	£16,000
External failure costs	£210,000

Workings

Number of estimated defective goods 10 million/1,000 x 3 = 30,000 units

	£
Appraisal costs – quality inspections	35,000
Internal failure costs – lost contribution on sales of seconds 4,000 x (£15 – £11)	16,000
External failure costs	
– replacement cost 30,000 x £10 x 70%	210,000
	261,000

• •

Task 8.5

Quality inspection costs	£340,000	– appraisal cost – explicit
Lost contribution from seconds		
5,200 units x (£200 – £108)	£478,400	– internal failure cost – explicit
Replacement of defective units		
1,000,000/2,000 x 60% x £120	£36,000	– external failure cost – explicit
Lost customers		
1,000,000/2,000 x 40% x (£200 - £120)	£16,000	– external failure cost – implicit

Task 8.6

Under traditional costing methods the costs of a product are only recorded and analysed once production of the product has begun. However, it is recognised that a large proportion of the costs of a product are incurred before production has started in the early stages of the product life cycle. Life cycle costing recognises all of these pre-production costs of the product such as:

- design costs
- prototyping
- programming
- process design
- equipment acquisition

The aim of life cycle costing is to ensure that all the costs of the product are accumulated over the whole of its life cycle in order to ensure that all costs are covered by revenue from the product.

Task 8.7

(a) The four general headings making up the cost of quality are as follows.

   (i)   Prevention costs
   (ii) Appraisal costs
   (iii) Internal failure costs
   (iv) External failure costs

(b) Examples of types of cost likely to be found in each category are as follows.

   (i)   Prevention costs. Maintenance of quality control equipment, training in quality control

   (ii) Appraisal costs. Inspection of goods inwards, inspection costs of in-house processing

   (iii) Internal failure costs. Losses from failure of purchased items, losses due to lower selling prices for sub-quality goods

   (iv) External failure costs. Costs of customer complaints section, cost of repairing products returned from customers

(c) Implications for the existing costing system

    (i) If there are fixed price contracts with guaranteed levels of quality there are likely to be few, if any, material price variances or material usage variances due to poor quality.

    (ii) The cost of labour will effectively become a fixed cost, the actual unit cost of labour simply depending on the volume produced. Labour efficiency variances could therefore be calculated but they will not reflect costs saved or excess wages paid. Labour rate variances are likely to be minimal if there is a guaranteed weekly wage.

    (iii) Predetermined standards conflict with the TQM philosophy of continual improvement.

    (iv) Continual improvements should alter prices, quantities of inputs and so on, whereas standard costing systems are best used in stable, standardised, repetitive environments.

    (v) Standard costing systems often incorporate a planned level of scrap in material standards. This is at odds with the TQM aim of 'zero defects'.

Results of these implications

    (i) There is less need for a standard costing system: variances are likely to be small or non-existent and, if incurred, non-controllable; the use of standards is inappropriate in a TQM environment.

    (ii) With the flexible work practices, capture of actual labour costs by individual jobs would be very difficult. Only material costs could be collected in the normal way. It is therefore unlikely that the full marginal cost of individual jobs could be collected.

(d) A cost saving not recorded in the existing costing system

With the introduction of a TQM system, the cost of having money tied up in high levels of inventory (stock) will be saved. This cost would not normally be captured by Barnet Ltd's existing costing system.

Note. A fuller answer has been given here than was required for assessment purposes.

Task 8.8

(a) **Background paper for meeting**

To: Jane Greenwood, Management Accountant

From: Assistant Management Accountant

Subject: Total quality management and the cost of quality

Date: xx/xx/xx

(i) The meaning of Total Quality Management

Total Quality Management (TQM) is a philosophy that guides every activity within a business. It is concerned with developing and sustaining a culture of continuous improvement which focuses on meeting customers' expectations.

One of the basic principles of TQM is therefore a dissatisfaction with the status quo: the belief that it is always possible to improve and so the aim should be to 'get it more right next time'. This involves the development of a commitment to quality by all staff and a programme of continuous learning throughout the entire organisation, possibly by empowering employees and making them responsible

The for the quality of production or by introducing quality circles.customer-centred approach of TQM hinges upon identifying the 'customers', focusing attention on them and then meeting their needs in terms of price, quality and timing. Organisations must therefore be customer-oriented rather than, as is traditionally the case, production-oriented.

One of the goals of TQM is to get it right first time. By continuously improving towards zero defects, the quality of the product delivered to the customer is improved. The quality of output depends on the quality of materials input, however, and so either extensive quality control procedures are needed at the point where goods are accepted and inspected or quality assurance schemes, whereby the supplier guarantees the quality of the goods supplied, must be in place.

A small proportion of mistakes are inevitable in any organisation but more often than not those mistakes have been 'designed' into the production process. Because TQM aims to get it right first time, however, quality and not faults must be designed into an organisation's products and operations from the outset. Quality control must therefore happen at the production design and production engineering stages of a product's life, as well as actually during production.

In summary, TQM involves getting it right first time and improving continuously.

(ii) Failure of the current accounting system to highlight the cost of quality

Traditionally, the costs of scrapped units, wasted materials and reworking have been subsumed within the costs of production by assigning the costs of an expected level of loss (a normal loss) to the costs of good production, while accounting for other costs of poor quality within production or marketing overheads. Such costs are therefore not only considered as inevitable but are not highlighted for management attention. Moreover, traditional accounting reports tend to ignore the hidden but real costs of excessive inventory (stock) levels (held to enable faulty material to be replaced without hindering production) and the facilities necessary for storing that inventory.

(iii)/(iv) **Explicit costs of quality**

There are four recognised categories of cost identifiable within an accounting system which make up the cost of quality.

(1) Prevention costs are the costs of any action taken to investigate,   prevent or reduce the production of faulty output. Included within this category are the costs of training in quality control and the cost of the design/development and maintenance of quality control equipment.

(2) Appraisal costs are the costs of assessing the actual quality achieved. Examples include the cost of the inspection of goods delivered and the cost of inspecting production during the manufacturing process.

(3) Internal failure costs are the costs incurred by the organisation when production fails to meet the level of quality required. Such costs include losses due to lower selling prices for sub-quality goods, the costs of reviewing product specifications after failures and losses arising from the failure of purchased items.

(4) External failure costs are the costs which arise outside the organisation (after the customer has received the product) due to failure to achieve the required level of quality. Included within this category are the costs of repairing products returned from customers, the cost of providing replacement items due to sub-standard products or marketing errors and the costs of a customer service department.

(v) **Quality costs not identified by the accounting system**

Quality costs which are not identified by the accounting system tend to be of two forms.

(1) Opportunity costs such as the loss of future sales to a customer dissatisfied with faulty goods.

(2) Costs which tend to be subsumed within other account headings such as those costs which result from the disruption caused by running out of inventory due to faulty purchases.

(b)   (i)   **Explicit cost of quality**

	£
Reworking (labour cost)	13,500
Customer support (contractors)	24,300
Store inspection costs	10,000
Cost of returns	4,500
	52,300

(ii) **Cost of quality not reported in the accounting records**

Opportunity cost (lost contribution from 100 X4s due to faulty circuit board) = £795 (W1) x 100 = £79,500.

Workings

(1)

		£
Labour (W2)		200
Printed circuit board (£120,000 ÷ 1,000)		120
Other material (£121,500 ÷ 900)		135
Marginal cost		455
Selling price		(1,250)
Contribution		795

(2)

	£
Total labour cost	193,500
Less cost of reworking	(13,500)
	180,000

Unit cost per good unit = £180,000 ÷ 900 = £200

Task 8.9

(a) The product life cycle is generally thought to split naturally into five separate stages:

- Development
- Launch
- Growth
- Maturity
- Decline

During the development and launch stage of the product's life there are large outgoings in terms of development expenditure, non-current (fixed) assets necessary for production, the building up of inventory (stock) levels and advertising and promotion expenses. It is likely that even after the launch sales will be quite low and the product will be making a loss at this stage.

If the launch of the product is successful then during the growth stage there will be fairly rapid increases in sales and a move to profitability as the costs of the earlier stages are covered. However, these sales increases are not likely to continue indefinitely.

In the maturity stage of the product demand for the product will probably start to slow down and become more constant. In many cases this is the stage where the product is modified or improved in order to sustain demand and this may then see a small surge in sales.

At some point in a product's life, unless it is a consumable item such as chocolate bars, the product will reach the end of its sales life, this is known as the decline stage. The market will have bought enough of the product and sales will decline. This is the point where the business should consider no longer producing the product.

(b) If the future demand for a product is to be forecast using time series analysis it is obviously important that the stage in the product life cycle that has been reached is taken into account. For example, if the trend is based upon the growth stage whereas in fact the product is moving into the maturity stage then the trend would show an overly optimistic forecast for sales.

Task 8.10

Target cost = market price – desired profit margin

= £50 – (£50 x 20%)

= £50 – £10

= £40

Task 8.11

Target cost = price – desired profit margin

= £25 – (£25 x 70%)

= £7.50 per unit

Sales price per unit = £250,000/10,000 = £25

SAMPLE ASSESSMENT 1
FINANCIAL PERFORMANCE

Time allowed: 2.5 hours

Section 1

Task 1.1

(a) **The following information has been calculated for the production of 1 unit of Beta**

Each unit will require 10 kilograms of material at a cost of £5.50 per kilogram
Each unit will require 5 hours of labour at a total cost of £40
Fixed overheads total £300,000 and the estimated output will be 2,500 units of Beta

Complete the standard cost card below.

1 unit of Beta	Quantity	Cost per unit £	Total cost £
Material			
Labour			
Fixed costs			
Total			

(b) An airline uses 250,000 kilograms of material to manufacture 500,000 airline meals.

Complete the following statement:

The standard quantity of each meal is ⬚ kgs.

Task 1.2

(a) **A company purchases 10,000 kilograms of material at a cost of £33,000. The standard cost per kilogram is £3. The total material price variance is:**

A   £0.30

B   £3,000

C   £300

D   £3.3

(b) **A company purchases 5,000 kilograms of material at a cost of £15,000. The budgeted production was 1,000 units which require 4,000 kilograms of material at a total standard cost of £14,000. The actual production was 1,000 units. The material usage variance is:**

A   £3.50

B   1,000 kilograms

C   £3,000

D   £3,500

(c) **A company uses the ideal standard to set budgets. How will this affect motivation?**

    A   An ideal standard is easy to meet and therefore motivation will be high

    B   It is impossible to meet an ideal standard and therefore staff will be motivated

    C   An ideal standard is the highest standard and therefore staff will always achieve it

    D   An ideal standard is set under perfect conditions and is difficult to meet, which can demotivate staff

(d) **A company expects to produce 12,000 units of X using 6,000 labour hours. The standard cost of labour is £14 per hour. If the actual output is 14,000 units, what is the total standard labour cost?**

    A   £168,000

    B   £98,000

    C   £196,000

    D   £84,000

Task 1.3

(a) **You have been given the following information:**

- Budgeted overheads are £600,000
- Budgeted output is 25,000 units
- Actual output is 30,000 units
- Actual overheads are £650,000

The fixed overhead volume variance is £ ☐ adverse/favourable

The fixed overhead expenditure variance is £ ☐ adverse/favourable

(b) **You have been given the following information:**

- Budgeted overheads are £50,000
- Budgeted output is 5,000 units and 50,000 labour hours
- Actual output is 4,000 units and 43,000 actual labour hours
- Actual overheads are £55,000

The fixed overhead efficiency variance is £ ☐ adverse/favourable

The fixed overhead capacity variance is £ ☐ adverse/favourable

Task 1.4

The following budgetary control report has been provided

	Budget		Actual	
Production (bottles)		10,000		11,000
Liquid shampoo	2,500 litres	£15,000	2,800 litres	£15,400
Plastic bottles	10,000 units	£2,000	11,300 units	£2,034
Direct labour	300 hours	£3,300	350 hours	£3,325
Fixed overheads		£7,000		£7,500
Total cost		£27,300		£28,259

The following variances have been calculated:

Fixed overhead expenditure	£500
Direct materials (shampoo) price	£1,400 F
Direct materials (bottles) price	£226 F
Direct materials (shampoo) usage	£300 A
Direct materials (bottles) usage	£60
Direct labour rate	£525
Direct labour efficiency	£220 A
Fixed overhead volume	£700 F

Calculate the standard cost of actual production, actual cost of actual production and the total variance. Insert the variances given above and the ones you have calculated in the appropriate parts of the operating statement.

	£	£	£
Budgeted/Standard cost for actual production			
Variances	Favourable	Adverse	
Direct materials (shampoo) price			
Direct materials (shampoo) usage			
Direct materials (bottles) price			
Direct materials (bottles) usage			
Direct labour rate			
Direct labour efficiency			
Fixed overhead expenditure			
Fixed overhead volume			
Total variance			
Actual cost of actual production			

Task 1.5

(a) The table below contains the last three months cost per kilogram for product Alpha.

January	February	March
Actual price was £3.40	Actual price was £3.30	Actual price was £3.50
Seasonal variation was 20p	Seasonal variation was 5p	Seasonal variation was 20p

Complete the following statement:

The trend in prices is an increase of £ [   ] per month.

(b) The table below contains the last three months total costs and quantities for product Alpha:

	January	February	March
Total cost	£100,000	£120,000	£125,000
Total quantity purchased	10,000 kg	11,000 kg	10,700 kg

The cost index for March based upon January being the base period of 100 is:

A   107
B   117
C   125
D   108

(c) The cost per unit of a product has increased from £36 in January to £40 in April. The cost per unit was £35 when the index was rebased to 100.

Which of the following statements is correct?

A   The cost index in April was 114 and the increase from January to April is 11.11%
B   The cost index in April was 111 and the increase from January to April is 11.11%
C   The cost index in April is 114 and the increase from January to April is 10%
D   The cost index in April is 111 and the increase from January to April is 10%

Task 1.6

Ufall has developed a skin treatment which claims to slow the ageing process. The product competes with a dozen other companies. Klineec is a major competitor and market leader, with over 60% of the market. You have been given the following information about Ufall and Klineec for the year ended 31 May 2010.

Income statement (Profit and loss account)	Ufall	Klineec
	£000	£000
Revenue (turnover)	9,000	44,000
Cost of production		
Direct (raw) materials	2,400	6,600
Direct labour	1,500	4,400
Fixed production overheads	1,200	6,000
Total cost of sales	5,100	17,000
Gross profit	3,900	27,000
Selling and distribution costs	1,000	2,000
Administration costs	750	1,500
Advertising costs	500	20,000
Net profit	1,650	3,500

Other information		Ufall	Klineec
Number of units sold (000)	Units	1,200	4,400
Net assets	(£000)	10,000	17,000

Calculate the following performance indicators for Ufall and Klineec:

(i)   **Selling price per unit**
(ii)   **Material cost per unit**
(iii)   **Labour cost per unit**
(iv)   **Fixed production overheads per unit**
(v)   **Gross profit margin**
(vi)   **Net profit margin**
(vii)   **Advertising costs as % of revenue**
(viii) **Return on net assets**

Give answers to two decimal places.

	Ufall	Klineec
Selling price per unit		
Material cost per unit		
Labour cost per unit		
Fixed production overheads per unit		
Gross profit margin		
Net profit margin		
Advertising cost as % of revenue		
Return on net assets		

Task 1.7

Alpha Limited manufactures an anti–ageing cream and is considering how it can be more environmentally friendly. Scientists have developed a new product to replace Alpha's existing anti-ageing cream; the new product is a solid bar and takes up less than 10% of the volume and weight of the existing product.

You have been given the following information.

- Current sales volume is 1.2 million units per annum and this is not expected to change.
- Current fixed production costs are £1.2 million.
- Current labour cost per unit is £1.25 which is completely variable.
- Current material cost per unit is £2 and is completely variable.
- Assume inventory (stock) levels are kept at zero.
- Variable cost of the new product will be £0.50 less per unit than the current cream.
- Selling price will be increased from £7.50 to £8.50.
- Fixed selling and distribution costs will reduce from £1,000,000 to £400,000.
- Additional investment in assets will be £3 million which will be depreciated at £500,000 per annum.
- All other costs will remain the same.

(a) **Calculate the total annual increase in profit by completing the table below.**

	Units	Price/cost £	Total £
Additional revenue			
Savings on variable costs			
Reduction in selling and distribution costs			
Additional depreciation			
Additional annual profit			

(b) **Complete the following sentence:**

The return on the additional investment (to two decimal places) is [   ]

(c) The marketing department is concerned that the volume of sales may not reach 1.2 million. The finance director has asked for the break even sales volume.

Complete the following sentences:

The fixed costs are £ [   ].

The contribution per unit is £ [   ] per unit.

The break even sales volume is [   ] units.

··

Task 1.8

Alpha Limited will be replacing some machines in the next year and needs to decide whether to purchase or lease the machines.

The discount factors you will need for task (a) and (b) are shown below.

Year	Discount factor 5%	Year	Discount factor 5%
0	1.00	3	0.864
1	0.952	4	0.823
2	0.907	5	0.784

(a) **Calculate the discounted lifecycle cost of purchasing the machine based upon the following:**

- Purchase price of £500,000
- Annual running costs of £40,000 for the next five years, paid annually in arrears
- A residual value of £200,000 at the end of the five years

Year	0	1	2	3	4	5
Cash flow £						
Discount factor						
Present value £						
Net present cost £						

(b) **Calculate the discounted lifecycle cost of leasing the machine for five years based upon the total annual costs of £125,000 paid annually in advance.**

Year	0	1	2	3	4
Lease costs £					
Discount factor					
Present value £					
Net present cost £					

(c) **Complete the following sentence:**

Based on the calculations it is best to purchase/lease the machine, which saves

£ [   ] .

Section 2

Task 2.1

You have been provided with the following operating statement for Golden Grind Limited which produces a ground coffee mix by mixing Arabica and Robusta coffee beans.

Variances	Favourable	Adverse
Direct materials (Arabica) price		£800
Direct materials (Arabica) usage	£2,250	
Direct materials (Robusta) price	£600	
Direct materials (Robusta) usage		£1,875

The Coffee Designer has given you the following information about Arabica and Robusta coffee beans:

- Arabica beans are a higher quality and provide a richer flavour.

- Robusta beans are considered lower quality and tend to be bitter in taste.

- The cost of Arabica beans is set by the market and recently the price has risen sharply due to a poor harvest. The purchaser has to take the price quoted on the market. The quality of the beans was as expected.

- The price of Robusta beans is set by the market and the price has recently fallen due to a good harvest. The purchaser has to take the price quoted on the market. The quality of the beans was as expected.

- A mixing machine broke down resulting in disruption to the process. This led to more Robusta beans being added and less Arabica beans being added to the mix.

- 6,000 kilograms of Robusta and 4,000 kilograms of Arabica beans were used to produce 9,500 kilograms of finished product. 500 kilograms were lost due to the machine breakdowns.

- The breakdown has been blamed on the loss of maintenance personnel due to a lower than market pay rise.

- In order to maintain the quality of the coffee blend, the percentage of Arabica beans should not fall below 50% of the weight of the blend.

Using this information, prepare a report to the Production Director to cover the following:

(a) **Provide possible reasons for the Arabica and Robusta variances by considering the following:**
   - Quality of the beans
   - Machine breakdowns
   - Mix of beans

(b) **Discuss if the company could have taken any action and, if so, what action could have been taken in respect of the:**
   - Quality of the beans, and
   - Machine breakdowns

To:	Subject:
From:	Date:

(a) Possible reasons for the variances

- Direct materials (Arabica) price variance

- Direct materials (Arabica) usage variance

- Direct materials (Robusta) price variance

- Direct materials (Robusta) usage variance

(b) Action which could have been taken

- Quality of beans

- Machines breakdown

Task 2.2

A division of Alpha Limited is developing a new product and a colleague has prepared forecast information based upon two scenarios. The forecast income statement (profit and loss account) and statement of financial position (balance sheet) for both scenarios is shown below:

- Scenario 1 is to set the price at £9 per unit with sales of 120,000 units each year.
- Scenario 2 is to set the price at £6 per unit with sales of 240,000 units each year.

Forecast Income statement	Scenario 1	Scenario 2
	£	£
Revenue (turnover)	1,080,000	1,440,000
Cost of production		
Direct (Raw) Materials	300,000	600,000
Direct Labour	120,000	192,000
Fixed Production overheads	360,000	360,000
Total cost of sales	780,000	1,152,000
Gross profit	**300,000**	**288,000**
Selling and distribution costs	74,000	122,000
Administration costs	50,000	50,000
Operating profit	**176,000**	**116,000**

	Scenario 1	Scenario 2
Gross profit margin	27.78%	20.00%
Operating profit margin	16.30%	8.06%
Direct materials as a percentage of turnover	27.78%	41.67%
Direct materials cost per unit	£2.50	£2.50
Direct labour cost per unit	£1.00	£0.80
Fixed production cost per unit	£3.00	£1.50

Draft a report for the Finance Director covering the following:

(a) An explanation of why the gross profit margins are different, referring to the following:
- Sales price
- Sales volume
- Materials
- Labour
- Fixed costs
- The dominant factor

(b) An explanation of why the net profit margins are different.

(c)   A recommendation, with reasons, as to which course of action to take.

To:	**Subject:**
From:	**Date:**

(a)   Why are the gross profit margins different?

- Sales Price / Sales Volume

- Materials

- Labour

- Fixed costs

- Which is the dominant factor and why?

(b)   Why are the net profit margins different?

(c)   Recommendation, with reasons, as to which course of action to take.

SAMPLE ASSESSMENT 1
FINANCIAL PERFORMANCE

ANSWERS

Section 1

Task 1.1

(a)

1 unit of Beta	Quantity	Cost per unit £	Total cost £
Material	10	5.50	55
Labour	5	8	40
Fixed costs	1 (accept 5 hours)	120 (24 per hour)	120
Total			215

(b)   0.50 kgs

Task 1.2

(a) **B**   £3,000

(b) **D**   £3,500

(c) **D**   An ideal standard is set under perfect conditions and is difficult to meet, which can demotivate staff.

(d) **B**   £98,000

Task 1.3

(a) The fixed overhead volume variance is £ 120,000 (F)

The fixed overhead expenditure variance is £ 50,000 (A)

(b) The fixed overhead efficiency variance is £ 3,000 (A)

The fixed overhead capacity variance is £ 7,000 (A)

Task 1.4

	£	£	£
Budgeted/Standard cost for actual production			**30,030**
Variances	Favourable	Adverse	
Direct materials (shampoo) price	1,400		
Direct materials (shampoo) usage		300	
Direct materials (bottles) price	226		
Direct materials (bottles) usage		60	
Direct labour rate	525		
Direct labour efficiency		220	
Fixed overhead expenditure		500	
Fixed overhead volume	700		
Total variance	2,851	1,080	**1,771**
Actual cost of actual production			**28,259**

....

Task 1.5

(a) The trend in prices is an increase of £ | 0.05 | per month.

(b) B   117

(c) A   The cost index in April was 114 and the increase from January to April is 11.11%

....

Task 1.6

	Ufall	Klineec
Selling price per unit	£7.50	£10.00
Material cost per unit	£2.00	£1.50
Labour cost per unit	£1.25	£1.00
Fixed cost per unit	£1.00	£1.36
Gross profit margin	43%	61%
Net profit margin	18%	8%
Advertising cost as % of turnover	5.6%	45.5%
Return on net assets	17%	21%

....

Task 1.7

(a)

	Units	Price/cost £	Total £
Additional revenue	1,200,000	1.00	1,200,000
Savings on variable costs	1,200,000	0.50	600,000
Reduction in selling and distribution costs			600,000
Additional depreciation			-500,000
Additional annual profit			1,900,000

(b) The return on the additional investment (to two decimal places) is 63.33%.

Working: Additional investment / Additional assets = £1,900,000/£3,000,000 = 63.33%

(c) The fixed costs are **£2.1 million**

Working: £1.2 million plus £400,000 plus additional depreciation of £500,000 =. £2.1 million

The contribution per unit is **£5.75** per unit.

Working: £8.50 less (3.25 – 0.50) = 8.50 – 2.75 = £5.75 per unit.

The break even sales volume is **365,218 units**.

Working: £2,100,000/£5.75 = 365,218 units (rounded up)

Task 1.8

(a)

Year	0	1	2	3	4	5
Cash Flow	£500,000	£40,000	£40,000	£40,000	£40,000	-£160,000
Discount factor	1	0.952	0.907	0.864	0.823	0.784
Present value	£500,000	£38,080	£36,280	£34,560	£32,920	-£125,440
NPC	£516,400					

(b)

Year	0	1	2	3	4
Lease costs	£125,000	£125,000	£125,000	£125,000	£125,000
Discount factor	1	0.952	0.907	0.864	0.823
Present value	£125,000	£119,000	£113,375	£108,000	£102,875
NPC	£568,250				

(c)   Based on the calculations it is best to **purchase** the machine, which saves **£51,850**.

Section 2

Task 2.1

To:	Production Director	Subject:	Reason for variances
From:	AAT student	Date:	xx/xx/xx

(a) **Possible reasons for the variances**

- **Direct materials (Arabica) price variance**

  The price variance for Arabica beans is £800 adverse. This is due to the market price of beans **increasing due to the poor harvest**, meaning there is lower supply, and so the price increases. The company **could not have taken any action as the market sets the price.**

- **Direct materials (Arabica) usage variance**

  The usage variance for Arabica beans is £2,250 favourable. This has been caused by the mixing process making an error and adding a greater amount of Robusta beans to the mix. The result is that the company has saved money because they have used less Arabica beans per kilogram of production, but the mix is outside of the range recommended to produce an acceptable quality blend. Therefore the customers may be unhappy.

  The company could have secured the maintenance personnel by paying a market rate.

- **Direct materials (Robusta) price variance**

  The price variance for Robusta beans is £600 favourable. This is due to the market price of beans decreasing as a result of a good harvest, meaning there is a larger supply, and so the price reduces. The company could not have taken any action as the market sets the price.

- **Direct materials (Robusta) usage variance**

  The usage variance is £1,875 adverse because the company used more beans than expected. This was because of the mixing machine breaking down.

(b) **Action which could have been taken**

- **Quality of beans**

  No action is necessary. As the quality was as expected, no action could be taken as quality is dependent on the harvest.

- **Machines breakdown**

  The information states that the low pay rise meant that maintenance staff left. One option would be to pay more to retain maintenance staff, or outsource to a reliable company.

Task 2.2

To: **Finance director**	Subject: **various**
From: **Accounting technician**	Date: **xx/xx/xx**

(a) **Why are the gross profit margins different?**

- **Sales price / sales volume**

  The sales price is higher under Scenario 1 which will result in an increase in the gross profit margin. However, the sales volume is half that of Scenario 2, which will reduce the margin if there are fixed costs because the fixed cost per unit will be higher.

- **Materials**

  The materials cost per unit is constant and therefore does not affect the gross profit margin. There is no economy of scale.

- **Labour**

  Labour cost per unit is £1 for Scenario 1 decreasing to £0.80 for Scenario 2. The more units that are produced, the lower the labour cost per unit. This will improve the margin for Scenario 2. It may be because of economies of scale in production or the learning effect.

- **Fixed costs**

  Fixed costs are constant in total, and so as the volume of production increases, the fixed cost per unit decreases. This will increase the margin.

- **Which is the dominant factor and why?**

  Scenario 2 sells twice as many units as Scenario 1, has the same material cost per unit, lower labour cost per unit, and lower fixed costs per unit. All of these would increase Scenario 2's margin. However, the margin is lower. This is due to the lower sales price per unit, which is the dominant factor.

(b) **Why are the net profit margins different?**

The net profit margins are different partly due to the reduction in gross profit for Scenario 2, and partly due to the increased sales and distribution costs in Scenario 2.

(c) **Recommendation, with reasons, as to which course of action to take**

Based purely on the forecast information Scenario 1 is the best option creating the largest return. However, the sales volume is lower than Scenario 2, and so the market share is lower. It may be worth setting the price lower to gain market share. Alternatively, what would be the demand if the price could be set approximately £8 per unit?

SAMPLE ASSESSMENT 2
FINANCIAL PERFORMANCE

Time allowed: 2.5 hours

SAMPLE ASSESSMENT 2

Section 1

Task 1.1

The following information has been calculated for the production of Alpha.

- Each unit will require 0.5 kilograms of material X1 at a cost of £7 per kilogram and 0.5 kilograms of material Y1 at a cost of £12 per kilogram.

- Each unit will require 2.5 hours of labour at a cost of £10 per hour.

- Fixed overheads total £250,000 and the overheads are absorbed on the basis of labour hours.

- Actual output was 49,000 units.

- Budgeted output is 50,000 units.

Complete the standard cost card below for Alpha

1 unit of Alpha	Quantity	Cost per unit £	Total £
Material X1			
Material Y1			
Labour		10	
Fixed overheads			
Total			

....

Task 1.2

Beta manufactures product XX20.

Beta operates a standard cost system in which:

- purchases of materials are recorded at standard cost
- direct material and direct labour costs are variable
- production overheads are fixed and absorbed on a labour hours basis

The budgeted activity and actual results for the month are as follows:

	Budget		Actual	
Production units (XX20)		200,000		190,000
Direct materials	1,000 litres	£9,000	1,000 litres	£8,500
Direct labour	400 hours	£6,000	360 hours	£5,760
Fixed overheads		£12,000		£13,000
Total cost		£27,000		£27,260

Calculate the following variances, if any.

Variance	Amount £	Adverse/Favourable
Direct material usage		
Direct material price		
Direct labour rate		
Direct labour efficiency		

Task 1.3A

Beta manufactures product GT1. Beta operates a standard cost system in which:

- purchases of materials are recorded at standard cost
- direct material and direct labour costs are variable
- production overheads are fixed and absorbed on a labour hours basis

The budgeted activity and actual results for the month are as follows:

	Budget		Actual	
Production units (GT1)		17,000		18,000
Direct materials	2,000 kg	£68,000	2,500 kg	£83,000
Direct labour	4,250 hours	£28,800	4,200 hours	£29,000
Fixed overheads		£104,125		£98,450
Total cost		£200,925		£210,450

Calculate the following variances, if any.

Variance	Amount £	Adverse/favourable
Fixed overhead capacity		
Fixed overhead expenditure		
Fixed overhead efficiency		

Task 1.3B

Information relating to the overheads for the period for Gamma is shown below:

Budgeted output is 15,000 units

Actual output was 15,700 units

Budgeted overheads are £300,000

Actual overheads were £320,000

Budgeted labour hours are 60,000

Actual labour hours were 58,000

Complete the following sentences.

The budgeted overhead absorption rate per hour is £ [ ]

The fixed overhead volume variance is [Adverse/Favourable]

Task 1.4A

The following budgetary control report has been provided together with the variances calculated below:

	Budget		Actual	
Production (units)		1,200		1,300
Direct materials	4,800 kg	£115,200	6,500 kg	£104,000
Direct labour	6,000 hours	£48,000	7,800 hours	£70,200
Fixed overheads		£15,000		£13,500
Total cost		£178,200		£187,700

Variance	Amount £
Direct material usage	£31,200 A
Direct materials price	£52,000
Fixed overhead expenditure	£1,500
Direct labour rate	£7,800
Direct labour efficiency	£10,400 A
Fixed overhead capacity	£4,500
Fixed overhead efficiency	£3,250 A

Calculate the standard cost for actual production, enter the individual variances in the appropriate columns, then calculate the total variance and the actual cost for actual production.

			£
Budgeted/standard cost for actual production			

Variance	Favourable £	Adverse £	
Direct materials price			
Direct materials usage			
Direct labour rate			
Direct labour efficiency			
Fixed overhead expenditure			
Fixed overhead capacity			
Fixed overhead efficiency			
Total variance			
Actual cost of actual production			

Task 1.4B

The fixed overhead capacity and efficiency variances will always be equal to which ONE of the following variances?

A   The total fixed overhead variance

B   The fixed overhead volume variance

C   The fixed overhead expenditure variance

D   The fixed overhead expenditure variance less the fixed overhead volume variance

Task 1.5A

Complete the table below by identifying the correct seasonal variation for each month.

	September	October	November	December
Cost per litre	£1.50	£1.45	£1.40	£1.80
Underlying trend	£1.40	£1.45	£1.50	£1.55
Seasonal variation £				

Task 1.5B

Complete the table to show the underlying cost and the forecast cost for each of the months October to December.

	July	August	September	October	November	December
Underlying cost per kg (£)	100	105	110			
Seasonal variation (£)	10	(5)	7	10	(8)	7
Actual cost/ forecast cost (£)	110	100	117			

Task 1.5C

The cost per unit of material AW10 was £120 per unit in January 20X1 and is £150 per unit in January 20X8.

Using January 20X1 as the base year the cost index for material AW10 as at January 20X8 is ....

The cost per unit has increased by........................percent between January 20X1 and 20X8.

Task 1.6

You have been provided with the following information for companies A and B.

Income statement	Company A	Company B
Sales volume	300,000	250,000
	£	£
Total sales revenue	9,000,000	10,000,000
Material costs	1,800,000	2,000,000
Labour costs	2,700,000	3,000,000
Fixed production costs	2,250,000	2,250,000
Total cost of sales	**6,750,000**	**7,250,000**
Gross profit	**2,250,000**	**2,750,000**
Selling and distribution costs	900,000	1,150,000
Administration costs	900,000	1,360,000
Net profit	**450,000**	**240,000**
Other information		
Total debt	2,812,500	1,500,000
Net assets	5,625,000	2,000,000
Inventory (stock) of finished goods	400,000	450,000

Calculate the following performance indicators for Company A and Company B. Give answers to two decimal places where appropriate.

	Company A	Company B
Selling price per unit		
Material cost per unit		
Labour cost per unit		
Fixed production cost per unit		
Gross profit margin %		
Net profit margin %		
Return on net assets %		
Inventory (stock) turnover in days		

Task 1.7A

Alpha Limited manufactures a product. The results for the previous period are shown in table below.

Alpha	Period 1
Production capacity	140,000
Unit produced and sold	100,000
	£
Revenue (turnover)	4,000,000
Costs	
Direct material	1,000,000
Direct labour	600,000
Fixed production costs	1,200,000
Gross profit	**1,200,000**
Fixed administration costs	300,000
Fixed selling and distribution costs	250,000
Net profit	**650,000**

Complete the following sentences.

The contribution per unit is £ [   ]

The break even sales volume (in whole units) is [   ] units.

The margin of safety (to two decimal places) is [   ] %.

Task 1.7B

In relation to Alpha Limited you have been given the following information.

- A marketing campaign is to be undertaken which will cost £300,000.
- Selling price will be reduced from £40 to £38.
- Current sales volume is 100,000 units per period and this is expected to increase to 125,000 units as a result of the campaign and reduction in sales price.
- All other fixed costs will remain unchanged.
- Labour cost per unit is completely variable.
- Material cost per unit is completely variable.
- Assume inventory (stock) levels are kept at zero.

Complete the following sentences:

The additional revenue will be £ [   ]

The additional contribution will be £ [   ]

The additional profit will be £ [   ]

Task 1.7C

Alpha Ltd's marketing department is concerned that the volume of sales may not reach 125,000 per period. The finance director has asked for the break even sales volume.

Complete the sentences below.

The fixed costs are £ [ ]

The contribution per unit is £ [ ]

The break even sales volume is [ ] units.

Task 1.8

Beta Limited is considering designing a new product, the JF007, and will use target costing to arrive at the target cost of the product. You have been given the following information:

- The price at which the product will be sold is £70.
- The company expects to sell 30,000 units at a price of £70.
- The fixed production cost is £360,000.
- The labour requirement is 1.5 hours at a cost of £18 per hour.
- The required profit margin is 30%.

Complete the sentences below.

The target total production cost per unit is £ [ ]

The target variable material cost per unit is £ [ ]

The contribution per unit is £ [ ]

The required volume of sales (assuming that the target variable cost per unit is met) to achieve a total profit of £800,000 is [ ] (to the nearest unit).

Section 2

Task 2.1

You have been provided with the following information for an organisation which manufactures product GG10. The following quarterly variances have been calculated by your colleague:

Variances	£
Direct materials price	4,000
Direct materials usage	8,000
Direct labour rate	8,000 A
Direct labour efficiency	14,000 F
Fixed overhead expenditure	6,000 A
Fixed overhead volume	10,000
Production information	
Budgeted units produced	100,000
Actual units produced	120,000

You have been given the following additional information:

- Your colleague has not indicated the sign for all variances so you will need to use your skill to identify the likely sign.

- A lower quality of materials was purchased and used.

- The material was tested and discovered to be of a lower grade. It has been estimated that this accounted for 30% of the usage variance.

- A special order was received resulting in overtime being used to fulfill the order. Also staff were given a pay rise which they all appreciated.

- One of the machines had to be repaired and it was established that the lower grade material caused more wear than expected.

Using this information, prepare a report to the Managing Director to cover an analysis of each variance by:

- **Identifying the sign for variances which are not already identified**
- **Explaining what the variance means**
- **Providing possible reasons for each variance**
- **Explaining any links between the variances**

| To: | | Subject: | |
| From: | | Date: | |

Analysis of variances

Direct materials price variance

Direct materials usage variance

Direct labour rate variance

Direct labour efficiency variance

Fixed overhead expenditure variance

Fixed overhead volume variance

Possible total effect of purchasing the lower grade material

Task 2.2

A division of Alpha Limited is developing a new product and a colleague has prepared forecast information based upon two scenarios. The forecast information for both scenarios is shown below:

- Scenario 1 is to set the price at £25 per unit with sales of 100,000 units each year.
- Scenario 2 is to set the price at £20 per unit with sales of 200,000 units each year.

Forecast information	Scenario 1	Scenario 2
	£	£
Revenue (turnover)	**2,500,000**	**4,000,000**
Cost of production		
Direct materials	800,000	1,600,000
Direct labour	500,000	800,000
Fixed production costs	800,000	800,000
Total cost of sales	**2,100,000**	**3,200,000**
Gross profit	**400,000**	**800,000**
Advertising costs	74,000	300,000
Administration costs	50,000	100,000
Net profit	**276,000**	**400,000**
Gross profit margin	16.00%	20.00%
Net profit margin	11.04%	10.00%
Return on net assets	8.00%	8.00%
Direct materials cost per unit	£8.00	£8.00
Direct labour cost per unit	£5.00	£4.00
Fixed production cost per unit	£8.00	£4.00

Draft a report for the Finance Director covering the following:

(a) An explanation of why the gross profit margins are different, referring to the following:

- sales price
- sales volume
- materials
- labour
- fixed production costs
- the dominant factor

(b) An explanation of why the net profit margins are different.

(c) A recommendation, with reasons, as to which course of action to take.

To:		Subject:	
From:		Date:	

(a) Why are the gross profit margins different?

Sales price / sales volume

Materials

Labour

Fixed production costs

Which is the dominant factor and why?

(b) Why are the net profit margins different?

(c) Recommendation, with reasons, as to which course of action to take

SAMPLE ASSESSMENT 2
FINANCIAL PERFORMANCE

ANSWERS

Section 1

Task 1.1

Working

Fixed overheads: £250,000/(50,000 x 2.5 hours) = £2 per unit

1 unit of Alpha	Quantity	Cost per unit £	Total £
Material X1	0.5	7	3.50
Material Y1	0.5	12	6.00
Labour	2.5	10	25.00
Fixed overheads (W)	2.5	2	5.00
Total			39.50

Task 1.2

Working

1   Standard cost per litre = £9,000/1,000 = £9. 190,000 units should have taken 190,000 x 1,000/200,000 = 950 litres, did take 1,000 litres, so the adverse usage variance is 1,000 – 950 = 50 x £9 = £450.

2   1,000 litres should have cost £9,000, did cost £8,500, so a £500 favourable price variance.

3   Standard rate per hour = £6,000/400 = £15. 360 hours at £15 should have cost £5,400, did cost £5,760, so the adverse rate variance is £360

4   190,000 units at standard efficiency should have taken 190,000 x 400/200,000 = 380 hours, did take 360 hours, so there is a favourable efficiency variance of 20 x £15 = £300.

Variance	Amount £	Adverse/favourable
Direct material usage (W1)	450	adverse
Direct material price (W2)	500	favourable
Direct labour rate (W3)	360	adverse
Direct labour efficiency (W4)	300	favourable

Task 1.3A

Working

1 Expenditure variance: £104,125 - £98,450 = £5,675 favourable

2 Standard absorption rate is £104,125/4,250 hours = £24.50 per hour. Standard hours for production of 18,000 units was 4,250/17,000 x 18,000 = 4,500 hours. It actually took 4,200 hours, so the favourable efficiency variance is 300 hours x £24.50 = £7,350.

3 While the budget planned activity of 4,250 hours, in fact only 4,200 hours were worked, so the adverse capacity variance is 50 x £24.50 = £1,225.

Variance	Amount £	Sign
Fixed overhead capacity (W3)	1,225	adverse
Fixed overhead expenditure (W1)	5,675	favourable
Fixed overhead efficiency (W2)	7,350	favourable

Task 1.3B

The budgeted overhead absorption rate per hour is £300,000/60,000 = **£5**

The fixed overhead volume variance is **favourable.** This is because the standard hours for actual production were 60,000/15,000 x 15,700 = 62,800 hours, while the budgeted hours were 60,000, so more overhead will have been absorbed than was budgeted.

Task 1.4A

Working

1 Standard cost is £178,200/1,200 x 1,300 = £193,050

2 Price variance: 6,500kg should have cost £115,200/4,800 kg = £156,000, but they did cost only £104,000, so there is a £52,000 favourable variance.

3 The standard labour rate was £48,000/6,000 hours = £8 per hour, so 7,800 hours should have cost £62,400. They cost £70,200, so the adverse rate variance is £7,800.

4 The favourable expenditure variance is £15,000 - £13,500 = £1,500.

5 Capacity variance: 1,800 more hours were worked than was budgeted. At a standard absorption rate of £15,000/6,000 = £2.50, there is therefore a favourable variance of £4,500.

			£
Budgeted/standard cost of actual production (W1)			193,050
Variance	**Favourable £**	**Adverse £**	
Direct material price (W2)	52,000		
Direct material usage		31,200	
Direct labour rate (W3)		7,800	
Direct labour efficiency		10,400	
Fixed overhead expenditure (W4)	1,500		
Fixed overhead capacity (W5)	4,500		
Fixed overhead efficiency		3,250	
Total variance			5,350
Actual cost of actual production			187,700

Task 1.4B

The fixed overhead capacity and efficiency variances will always be equal to the **fixed overhead volume variance**

Task 1.5A

	September	October	November	December
Cost per litre	£1.50	£1.45	£1.40	£1.80
Underlying trend	£1.40	£1.45	£1.50	£1.55
Seasonal variation	£0.10	£0	(£0.10)	£0.25

Task 1.5B

	July	August	September	October	November	December
Underlying cost per kg (£) – add £5 per month	100	105	110	115	120	125
Seasonal variation (£)	10	(5)	7	10	(8)	7
Actual cost/ forecast cost (£)	110	100	117	125	112	132

Task 1.5C

The cost per unit of material AW10 was £120 per unit in January 20X1 and is £150 per unit in January 20X8.

Using January 20X1 as the base year the cost index for material AW10 as at January 20X8 is **125**

The cost per unit has increased by **25**   percent between January 20X1 and 20X8.

Task 1.6

	Company A £	Company B £
Selling price per unit – revenue/volume	30	40
Material cost per unit – material cost/volume	6	8
Labour cost per unit – labour cost/volume	9	12
Fixed production cost per unit – cost/volume	7.50	9
Gross profit margin – gross profit/revenue x 100%	25%	27.5%
Net profit margin – net profit/revenue x 100%	5%	2.4%
Return on net assets – net profit/net assets x 100%	8%	12%
Inventory (stock) turnover in days – inventory/cost of sales x 365 days	21.63	22.66

Task 1.7A

The contribution per unit is **£24** ((£4,000,000 – £1,000,000 – £600,000)/100,000 units).

The break even sales volume (in whole units) is **72,917** units ((£1,200,000 + £300,000 + £250,000)/£24)

The margin of safety (to two decimal places) is **27.08**% ((100,000 – 72,917)/100,000 x 100%).

....

Task 1.7B

The additional revenue will be **£750,000** (125,000 x £38) – (100,000 x £40) = £750,000.

The additional contribution will be **£350,000** (125,000 x (£24 – (£40 – £38))) – (100,000 x £24).

The additional profit will be **£50,000** (£350,000 – £300,000 marketing).

....

Task 1.7C

The fixed costs are **£2,050,000** (£1,200,000 + £300,000 + £250,000 + £300,000).

The contribution per unit is **£22** (£24 – (£40 – £38).

The break even sales volume is **93,182** units (£2,050,000/£22, rounded up).

....

Task 1.8

(a) The target total production cost per unit is **£49** (£70 x70%)

(b) The target variable material cost per unit is **£10** (Total target cost: (£49 x 30,000 units) – £360,000 – (1.5 x £18 x 30,000 units) = £300,000, so with 30,000 units the target cost per unit is £10)

(c) The contribution per unit is **£33** (£70 – £10 – (1.5 x £18))

(d) The required volume of sales (assuming that the target variable cost per unit is met) to achieve a total profit of £800,000 is **35,152** (to the nearest unit). This is target profit £800,000 + fixed costs £360,000 divided by the contribution per unit of £33.

....

Section 2

Task 2.1

To: Finance Director	Subject: Analysis of variances
From: An Accountant	Date: XX/XX/XXXX

Direct materials price variance

The variance was £4,000 favourable. This means that the price was lower than expected. This is probably due to the purchase of a lower quality product, which may result in more wastage. The price variance is often linked to the usage variance. The usage variance can also be affected by other factors like the skill or the motivation of the labour force or the quality of the machines. The variance appears to be good but the lower quality has been estimated to have caused £2,400 (30% of £8,000) of the adverse usage variance, the result being a net gain of £1,600 (£4,000F less £2,400A).

Direct materials usage variance

The usage variance was £8,000 adverse. This means that more material was used than expected. This appears to support the issue with material quality but may also be due to the machinery problems which also appear to link back to the lower grade materials. It appears that there is a strong link between the usage variance and the price variance.

Direct labour rate variance

The variance was £8,000 adverse which means a higher rate was paid than expected. This may be in part due to the overtime payments and in part due to the pay rise. Overtime appears to be due to the special order but may also be due to the machine breakdowns causing loss of production.

Direct labour efficiency variance

The variance is £14,000 favourable which means fewer hours were used than expected. It appears that in spite of the lower grade material and the machine repairs labour still performed better than planned. It may be that with the better quality material this variance would have been even more favourable. Perhaps the overtime payments and also the pay rise motivated the staff.

Fixed overhead expenditure variance

The variance was £6,000 adverse. This means the actual costs were higher than expected. This appears to be due to the machine problems caused by the lower grade materials. There is possibly a strong link between the expenditure variance and material price variance.

Fixed overhead volume variance

The variance was £10,000F. This means the actual volume was more than expected. This has been caused by the special order. This means that more overhead has been absorbed than expected.

Possible total effect of purchasing the lower grade material

It appears that the lower quality material caused adverse variances for material usage and overhead expenditure and could also have caused some of the labour rate variance. The effect could have been as high as 2,400A for usage, 6,000A for overheads and a proportion of the 8,000A labour rate. The total effect could be as high as 16,400A less the 4,000F = 12,400A.

Task 2.2

To:	Finance Director	Subject:	Scenario analysis
From:	An Accountant	Date:	XX/XX/XXXX

(a) Why are the gross profit margins different?

Sales price / sales volume

The sales price is higher under S1 (£25 compared with £20) which will result in an increase in the gross profit margin, however the sales volume of S1 is half that of S2, which will reduce the margin for S1 if there are fixed costs, because the fixed cost per unit will be higher.

Materials

The materials cost per unit is constant and therefore does not affect the gross profit margin. There is no planned economy of scale.

Labour

Labour cost per unit is £5 for S1 decreasing to £4 for S2. The more units that are produced the lower the labour cost per unit. This will improve the margin for S2. There appear to be planned economies of scale in production as a result of the learning effect.

Fixed production costs

Fixed costs are constant in total therefore as the volume of production increases the fixed cost per unit reduces from £8 per unit under S1 to £4 per unit under S2. This will increase the margin for S2.

Which is the dominant factor and why?

S2 sells twice as many units as S1 and has the same material cost per unit, lower labour cost per unit and lower fixed costs per unit. All of these would increase S2's margin. However, the sales price per unit is lower by 20% which would reduce the margin for S2. Therefore the dominant factor is the additional sales volume generated under S2.

(b) Why are the net profit margins different?

The net profit margins are different due to the flow through of the gross profit margin and it could be expected that S2 would have the better net margin. However, there is a very large increase in advertising costs from £74,000 to £300,000 when moving from S1 to S2. This is probably necessary to stimulate demand together with the cut in price. The advertising costs have eroded the gross margin to leave a lower net margin under S2. The administration costs have also doubled which may be to cover the additional work as demand doubles.

(c) Recommendation, with reasons, as to which course of action to take

Based purely on the forecast information S1 is the best option creating the greater net profit margin. However, the sales volume is lower than S2 and therefore the market share is lower. It may be worth setting the price lower to gain market share. However, there is a risk that the additional advertising costs do not yield the expected increase in sales volume.

PRACTICE ASSESSMENT 1
FINANCIAL PERFORMANCE

Time allowed: 2.5 hours

Section 1

Task 1.1

RD Ltd manufactures rubberised asphalt and operates a standard costing system.

The standard cost card for the coming month is being prepared and you have been given the following information.

- 50 tonnes of CR materials will be transferred from the CR Division of the company at a cost of £474 per tonne.

- 200 tonnes of asphalt material will be purchased at a cost of £150 per tonne.

- Labour required to produce 250 tonnes of output is 800 hours.

- Labour cost is £10 per hour.

- Fixed running costs of the machines are £150,000 per month.

- Budgeted production is 250 tonnes per month.

- Fixed production overheads are absorbed on the basis of tonnes.

Complete the standard cost card for the production of 250 tonnes of rubberised asphalt.

		Quantity	Unit price £	Total cost £
CR materials	tonnes			
Asphalt	tonnes			
Direct labour	hours			
Fixed production overheads	tonnes			_____
Standard cost				_____

Task 1.2

The budgeted activity and actual results for a business for the month of May 20X8 are as follows:

		Budget			Actual
Production (tonnes)		200			210
Direct labour	600 hours	£4,800	600 hours		£5,100

Complete the following sentences:

The standard labour rate per hour is £ [   ] per hour.

The standard labour hours for actual production is [   ] hours.

The direct labour rate variance is £ [   ] (Adverse/Favourable).

The direct labour efficiency variance is £ [   ] (Adverse/Favourable).

Task 1.3

A business has a single product into which fixed overheads are absorbed on the basis of labour hours. The standard cost card shows that fixed overheads are to be absorbed on the basis of 8 labour hours per unit at a rate of £10.00 per hour. The budgeted level of production is 100,000 units.

The actual results for the period were that fixed overheads were £7,800,000 and that the actual hours worked were 820,000 and the actual units produced were 98,000.

Calculate the following variances:

	Variance £	Adverse/Favourable
Fixed overhead expenditure variance		
Fixed overhead volume variance		
Fixed overhead efficiency variance		
Fixed overhead capacity variance		

Task 1.4

You have been given an equation and information to estimate the cost of a raw material for January and February 20X9.

The equation is $Y = a + bX$, where:

- X is the time period in months
- the value for X in November 20X8 is 29
- the value for X in December 20X8 is 30
- Y is the cost of the raw material
- the constant "a" is 9 and constant "b" is 0.1

Complete the table to calculate the expected price of the raw material per kilogram for January and February 20X9.

January 20X9	£
February 20X9	£

Task 1.5

HM Ltd is considering purchasing a new machine to reduce the labour time taken to produce one of its products. The machine would cost £300,000. The labour time would be reduced from five hours to two hours without compromising quality and the failure rates will remain at zero.

The discount factors you will need are shown below.

Year	Discount factor 5%
0	1.000
1	0.952
2	0.907
3	0.864
4	0.823
5	0.784

(a) **Calculate the discounted lifecycle cost of the machine based upon the following:**

   (i)   purchase price of £300,000

   (ii) annual running costs of £30,000 for the next 5 years

   (iii) a residual value of £50,000 at the end of the 5 years

Year	0	1	2	3	4	5
	£'000	£'000	£'000	£'000	£'000	£'000
Purchase price						
Running cost						
Residual value	___	___	___	___	___	___
Net cost	___	___	___	___	___	___
Discount factor						
Present cost						

Net Present Cost = £ [   ]

The discounted lifecycle cost of the machine is £ [   ]

(b) **Calculate the discounted labour savings based upon annual production of 5,000 units, a three hour saving per unit and a labour rate of £7 per hour.**

Year	0	1	2	3	4	5
	£'000	£'000	£'000	£'000	£'000	£'000
Labour cost Saving						
Discount factor						
Present value						

Net Present Labour Cost Saving = £ [   ]

The discounted labour savings are £ [   ]

Task 1.6

A company imports tea from India and the historical cost per kilogram is shown below.

	June X7 £	July X7 £	Aug X7 £	Sept X7 £	Oct X7 £	Nov X7 £
Cost per kg of tea	4.95	4.97	4.99	5.05	5.08	5.10

(a) The price per kilogram at January 20X7 was £4.80.

Convert the costs per kilogram for June and November to index numbers using January 20X7 as the base year.

June cost	
November cost	

(b) It is expected that the index number for tea for January 20X8 will be 108.25.

What is the expected cost per kilogram for January 20X8?

A   £5.52

B   £5.36

C   £5.20

D   £5.40

(c) **The percentage increase in the price of tea from January 20X7 to January 20X8 is:**

A   8.33%

B   7.69%

C   5.80%

D   5.58%

....

Task 1.7

The activity levels and related production costs for the last four months of 20X8 for a business have been as follows:

	Activity level units	Production cost £
September	34,000	310,000
October	30,000	301,000
November	32,000	315,000
December	28,000	280,000

Complete the following sentences:

(a) The fixed element of the production costs is £ [   ] .

The variable element of the production costs per unit is £ [   ] .

(b) **Complete the table to show the estimated production costs at each of the levels of production.**

Level of production – units	Production cost £
31,000	
36,000	

....

Task 1.8

A business sells a single product and has budgeted sales of 130,000 units for the next period. The selling price per unit is £56 and the variable costs of production are £36. The fixed costs of the business are £2,000,000.

Complete the following sentences:

The breakeven point in units is [   ] units.

The margin of safety in units is [   ] units.

The margin of safety as a percentage of budgeted sales is [   ] %.

....

Section 2

Task 2.1

HE Ltd has been reviewing the quality of the solar panels that it produces and has engineered two new products, the SP2000 and the SP3000.

The SP2000 is a low quality product with an economic life of 5 years. The SP3000 is a high quality product with an economic life of 20 years.

The Sales Director has provided information about the expected demand and price for the SP2000 and SP3000 for the coming year.

- SP2000 will be priced at £200 per panel and demand is expected to be around 9,000 units per year.

- SP3000 will be priced at £300 per panel and demand is expected to be around 5,000 units per year.

Forecast income statement (profit and loss account)

	SP2000	SP3000
Volume	9,000 units	5,000 units
	£	£
Revenue (turnover)	1,800,000	1,500,000
Cost of production		
Direct materials (glass)	540,000	300,000
Direct labour	126,000	175,000
Fixed production overheads	120,000	120,000
Total cost of sales	786,000	595,000
Gross profit	**1,014,000**	**905,000**
Selling and distribution costs	400,000	400,000
Administration costs	200,000	200,000
Operating profit	**414,000**	**305,000**

Extracts from the forecast statement of financial position (balance sheet)

	£	£
Inventory (stock) of material (glass)	60,000	60,000
Inventory of finished goods	NIL	NIL
Net assets	2,014,000	1,905,000

(a) **Complete the table to calculate the following performance indicators for BOTH products.**

	SP2000	SP3000
Gross profit margin		
Operating profit margin		
Direct materials cost per unit		
Direct labour cost per unit		
Fixed production overheads cost per unit		
Return on net assets		
Raw materials inventory turnover in days		

(b) Draft a report for the Finance Director covering the following:

(i) an explanation of why the gross profit margin is different for each product. Your answer should refer to the following and explain their effect on the gross profit margin:

– sales price per unit

– materials, labour and fixed cost per unit

(ii) an assessment of the return on net assets for each product.

From: A Student

To: Finance Director

Sent: 1 December 20X8

Subject: Performance indicators

(i) **Gross profit margin**

(ii) **Return on net assets**

Task 2.2

You are employed as a financial analyst at Drampton plc, a computer retailer. One of your duties is to prepare a standard costing reconciliation statement for the finance director.

The company sells two types of computer, personal computers (PCs) for individual use and servers for large organisations. PCs are sold by advertising in newspapers. Customers telephone Drampton to place an order and the telephone call is answered by trained operators. Drampton pays the cost of the telephone call. The total standard cost of one phone call is shown below.

Standard cost of one call			
Expense	Quantity	Cost	Cost per call
			£
Telephone cost	1 unit	£0.07 per unit	0.07
Operators' wages	6 minutes	£7.00 per hour	0.70
Fixed overheads [1]	6 minutes	£6.50 per hour	0.65
Standard cost of one telephone call			1.42
[1] Fixed overheads are based on budgeted operator hours.			

Drampton's finance director gives you the following information for the three months ended 31 May 20X8.

- Budgeted number of calls — 900,000 calls
- Actual number of calls — 1,000,000 calls

• Actual expenses	Quantity	Cost £
Telephone cost	1,200,000 units	79,200
Operators' wages	114,000 hours	877,800
Fixed overheads		540,400
Actual cost of actual operations		1,497,400

(a) **Calculate the following information.**

    (i)   Actual telephone cost per unit

    (ii) Actual hourly wage rate of operators

    (iii) Standard number of operator hours for 1,000,000 calls

    (iv) Budgeted cost of fixed overheads for the three months ended 31 May 20X8

    (v) Budgeted number of operator hours for the three months ended 31 May 20X8

    (vi) Standard cost of actual operations

(b) Using the data given and your answers to part (a), calculate the following variances.

   (i)   Price variance for telephone calls

   (ii)   Usage variance for telephone calls

   (iii) Labour rate variance for the telephone operators

   (iv) Labour efficiency variance for the telephone operators

   (v)   Fixed overhead expenditure variance

   (vi) Fixed overhead volume variance

   (vii) Fixed overhead capacity variance

   (viii) Fixed overhead efficiency variance

(c) Prepare a statement for the three months ended 31 May 20X8 reconciling the standard cost of actual operations to the actual cost of actual operations.

Reconciliation statement – 3 months ended 31 May 20X8			
			£
Standard cost of actual operations			
	£	£	
Variances	(F)	(A)	
Price for telephone calls			
Usage for telephone calls			
Labour rate			
Labour efficiency			
Fixed overhead expenditure			
Fixed overhead capacity			
Fixed overhead efficiency			
Actual cost of actual operations			

PRACTICE ASSESSMENT 1
FINANCIAL PERFORMANCE

ANSWERS

Section 1

Task 1.1

Standard cost card for production of 250 tonnes of rubberised asphalt:

		Quantity	Unit price	Total cost
			£	£
CR material	tonnes	50	474	23,700
Asphalt	tonnes	200	150	30,000
Direct labour	hours	800	10	8,000
Fixed production overheads	tonnes	250	600	150,000
Standard cost				211,700

Task 1.2

The standard labour rate per hour is **£8** per hour.

The standard labour hours for actual production is **630** hours.

The direct labour rate variance is **£300 Adverse**

The direct labour efficiency variance is **£240 Favourable**

Workings

Standard labour rate per hour	=	budgeted labour cost / budgeted labour hours
	=	£4,800 / 600
	=	£8 per hour
Standard labour hours for actual production	=	standard labour hour per tonne x actual production
	=	600 hours/200 tonnes x 210 tonnes
	=	630 hours

Direct labour rate variance

	£
Actual hours at standard rate (600 x £8)	4,800
Actual hours at actual rate	5,100
Labour rate variance	300 Adv

Direct labour efficiency variance

	£
Standard hours for actual production at the standard rate	
3 x 210 x £8	5,040
Actual hours for actual production at the standard rate 600 x £8	4,800
Labour efficiency variance	240 Fav

Task 1.3

	Variance £	Adverse/Favourable
Fixed overhead expenditure variance	200,000	Favourable
Fixed overhead volume variance	160,000	Adverse
Fixed overhead efficiency variance	360,000	Adverse
Fixed overhead capacity variance	200,000	Favourable

Workings

Fixed overhead expenditure variance

	£
Budgeted fixed overhead 100,000 units x 8 hours x £10.00	8,000,000
Actual fixed overhead	7,800,000
Expenditure variance	200,000 (F)

Fixed overhead volume variance

	£
Standard hours for actual production @ standard OAR 98,000 units x 8 hours x £10.00	7,840,000
Standard hours for budgeted production @ standard OAR 100,000 units x 8 hours x £10.00	8,000,000
Volume variance	160,000 (A)

Fixed overhead efficiency variance

	£
Standard hours for actual production @ standard OAR 98,000 x 8 hours x £10.00	7,840,000
Actual hours @ standard OAR 820,000 x £10.00	8,200,000
Efficiency variance	360,000 (A)

Fixed overhead capacity variance

	£
Actual hours @ standard OAR 820,000 x £10.00	8,200,000
Budgeted hours @ standard OAR 100,000 x 8 x £10.00	8,000,000
Capacity variance	200,000 (F)

Task 1.4

January 20X9	£12.10
February 20X9	£12.20

Workings

In January:

a = 9

b = 0.1

X = 31

Therefore Y = 9 + (31 x 0.1) = £12.10 per kilogram

In February:

a = 9

b = 0.1

X = 32

Therefore Y = 9 + (32 x 0.1) = £12.20 per kilogram

Task 1.5

(a)

Year	0	1	2	3	4	5
	£'000	£'000	£'000	£'000	£'000	£'000
Purchase price	300					
Running cost		30	30	30	30	30
Residual value	—	—	—	—	—	(50)
Net cost	300	30	30	30	30	(20)
Discount factor	1.000	0.952	0.907	0.864	0.823	0.784
Present cost	300	28.560	27.210	25.920	24.690	(15.680)

Net Present Cost = £390,700

The discounted lifecycle cost of the machine is £390,700.

(b)

Year	0	1	2	3	4	5
	£'000	£'000	£'000	£'000	£'000	£'000
Labour cost Saving (W1)	0	105	105	105	105	105
Discount factor	1.000	0.952	0.907	0.864	0.823	0.784
Present value		99.960	95.235	90.720	86.415	82.320

Net Present Labour Cost Saving = £454,650

The discounted labour savings are £454,650

Working

3 hours saving per unit x 5000 units x £7 = £105,000

Task 1.6

(a)

June cost	103.13
November cost	106.25

June = $\dfrac{£4.95}{£4.80} \times 100 = 103.13$

November = $\dfrac{£5.10}{£4.80} \times 100 = 106.25$

(b) C   January X8 cost = $\dfrac{£4.80 \times 108.25}{100} = £5.20$

(c) A   Percentage increase = $\dfrac{£5.20 - £4.80}{£4.80} \times 100$

$= 8.33\%$

....

Task 1.7

(a) The fixed element of the production costs is £140,000

The variable element of the production costs per unit is £5

Workings

	Activity level	Cost £
December (lowest)	28,000	280,000
September (highest)	34,000	310,000
Increase	6,000	30,000

Variable element = £30,000/6,000

$= £5$ per unit

	£
December:	
Variable element £5 x 28,000 units	140,000
Fixed element (bal fig)	140,000
Total cost	280,000

(b)

Level of production – units	Production cost - £
31,000	295,000
36,000	320,000

Workings

(i)   Production level of 31,000 units:

	£
Variable cost £5 x 31,000	155,000
Fixed cost	140,000
Total cost	295,000

(ii)   Production level of 36,000 units:

	£
Variable cost £5 x 36,000	180,000
Fixed cost	140,000
Total cost	320,000

....

Task 1.8

The breakeven point in units is 100,000 units

The margin of safety in units is 30,000 units

The margin of safety as a percentage of budgeted sales is 23%

Workings

$$\text{Breakeven point} = \frac{£2,000,000}{£56 - £36}$$

$$= 100,000 \text{ units}$$

Margin of safety (units) = Budgeted sales – breakeven sales

$$= (130,000 - 100,000) \text{ units}$$

$$= 30,000 \text{ units}$$

$$\text{Margin of safety (\% budgeted sales)} = \frac{130,000 - 100,000}{130,000} \times 100\%$$

$$= 23\%$$

....

Section 2

Task 2.1

(a)

	SP2000	SP3000
Gross profit margin	56.33%	60.33%
Operating profit margin	23.00%	20.33%
Direct materials cost per unit	£60.00	£60.00
Direct labour cost per unit	£14.00	£35.00
Fixed production overheads cost per unit	£13.33	£24.00
Return on net assets	20.56%	16.01%
Raw materials inventory turnover in days	40.56 days	73.00 days

Workings

	SP2000	SP3000
Note all monetary amounts in '000 for (i) and (ii)		
(i) = Gross Profit/Turnover × 100	Gross profit margin (1,014/1,800) × 100 = 56.33%	(905/1,500) × 100 = 60.33%
(ii) = Operating Profit/Turnover × 100	Operating profit margin (414/1,800) × 100 = 23.00%	(305/1,500) × 100 = 20.33%
(iii) = Direct materials cost/sales units	Direct materials cost per unit £540,000/9,000 = £60.00	£300,000/5,000=£60.00
(iv) = Direct labour cost/sales units	Direct labour cost per unit £126,000/9,000 = £14.00	£175,000/5,000=£35.00
(v) = Fixed prod'n o/hds cost/sales units	Fixed production overheads cost per unit £120,000/9,000 = £13.33	£120,000/5,000=£24.00
(vi) = Operating profit / Net assets × 100	Return on net assets £414,000/£2,014,000 × 100 = 20.56%	£305,000/£ 1,905,000 × 100 = 16.01%

(vii) = (inventory of material/Direct materials) × 365

Inventory Turnover

£60,000/£540,000 × 365

= 40.56 days

£60,000/£300,000 × 365

= 73.00 days

(b)

From: A Student

To: Finance Director

Sent: 1 December 20X8

Subject: Performance indicators

(i) **Gross profit margin**

The gross margin for the SP3000 is higher than the SP2000 by 4%.

This difference can be explained by differences in the selling price per unit and the cost of production of each unit.

The selling price of the SP3000 is £300 per unit whereas the selling price of the SP2000 is £200 per unit. If the cost of production for both products was the same then the SP3000 would have a higher gross margin.

The cost of production of the two products should be compared:

- The direct material cost of glass is constant at £60 per unit and so does not affect the margin.

- The direct labour cost per unit is much higher for the SP3000. This will reduce the gross margin for the SP3000.

- The fixed costs per unit are also higher for the SP3000 because less volume is produced (£24 per unit as opposed to £13.33 per unit for SP2000). Again this will reduce the margin for the SP3000.

The higher unit selling price of the SP3000 more than outweighs the additional costs per unit and hence the SP3000 has a higher gross margin.

(ii) **Return on net assets**

The SP2000 has a higher return on net assets than the SP3000 because its operating profits are larger relative to its net assets. Thus it generates an additional £109,000 but only uses an additional £109,000 of net assets.

Task 2.2

(a) (i) Actual telephone cost per unit = total actual cost ÷ total actual units = £79,200 ÷ 1,200,000 = £0.066

(ii) Actual hourly wage rate of operators = actual total cost of operators' wages ÷ actual hours worked = £877,800 ÷ 114,000 hours = £7.70

(iii) Standard number of operator hours per call = 6 mins = 0.1 hr

Standard number of operator hours for 1,000,000 calls = 0.1 hr × 1,000,000 = 100,000 hours

(iv) Fixed overheads are based on budgeted operator hours.

Budgeted number of calls	= 900,000
Budgeted number of operator hours	= 900,000 × 0.1 hour = 90,000
Fixed overhead absorption rate	= £6.50 per hour
Budgeted cost of fixed overheads	= 90,000 hours × £6.50 per hour
	= £585,000

(v) See (iv) above

(vi) Standard cost of actual operations = actual number of calls × standard cost per call = 1,000,000 × £1.42 = £1,420,000

(b) (i) **Price variance for telephone calls**

	£
1,200,000 units should have cost (× £0.07)	84,000
but did cost	79,200
	4,800 (F)

(ii) **Usage variance for telephone calls**

1,000,000 calls should have used (× 1 unit)	1,000,000 units
but did use	1,200,000 units
Variance in units	200,000 units (A)
× standard rate per unit	× £0.07
	£14,000 (A)

(iii) **Labour rate variance for the telephone operators**

	£
114,000 hours should have cost (× £7.00)	798,000
but did cost	877,800
	79,800 (A)

(iv) **Labour efficiency variance for the telephone operators**

1,000,000 calls should have taken [from (a) (iii)]	100,000 hrs
but did take	114,000 hrs
Variance in hours	14,000 hrs (A)
× standard rate per hour	× £7.00
	£98,000 (A)

(v) Fixed overhead expenditure variance

	£
Budgeted expenditure (from a)iv))	585,000
Actual expenditure	540,400
	44,600 (F)

(vi) Fixed overhead volume variance

	£
Budgeted number of calls	900,000
Actual number of calls	1,000,000
Variance in calls	100,000 (F)
× standard fixed overhead per call	× £0.65
	65,000 (F)

(vii) Fixed overhead capacity variance

Budgeted operator hours (from a)v))	90,000 hrs
Actual operator hours	114,000 hrs
Variance in units	24,000 hrs (F)
× standard absorption rate per hour	× £6.50
	£156,000 (F)

(viii) Fixed overhead efficiency variance

Labour efficiency variance (as overheads are absorbed on a labour hour basis)(from b)iv))	14,000 hrs (A)
× standard absorption rate per hour	× £6.50
	£91,000 (A)

(c) Reconciliation statement – 3 months ended 31 May 20X8

			£
Standard cost of actual operations (from (a)(vi))			1,420,000
	£	£	
Variances	(F)	(A)	
Price for telephone calls	4,800		
Usage for telephone calls		14,000	
Labour rate		79,800	
Labour efficiency		98,000	
Fixed overhead expenditure	44,600		
Fixed overhead capacity	156,000		
Fixed overhead efficiency		91,000	
	205,400	282,800	77,400 (A)
Actual cost of actual operations			1,497,400

PRACTICE ASSESSMENT 2
FINANCIAL PERFORMANCE

Time allowed: 2.5 hours

Section 1

Task 1.1

The bagging division of a tea company operates a standard costing system. The standard cost card for the coming months is being prepared and you have been provided with the following information.

- Loose tea is expected to cost £5 per kilogram
- 1,000 tea bags require 3 kilograms of loose tea
- Tea bags cost 0.6 pence per bag
- One machine can package 5,000 bags per hour and requires one operator who costs £10 per hour
- Budgeted labour hours are 4,000 per month
- Fixed production overheads are £200,000 per month
- Budgeted production is 20,000 batches of 1,000 tea bags per month
- Fixed production overheads are absorbed on the basis of direct labour hours

Prepare the standard cost card for the production of 1,000 tea bags.

Standard cost card for 1,000 tea bags	£
Direct materials	
Direct materials	
Direct labour	
Fixed overhead	
Total standard cost	

Task 1.2

A business produces one product which requires the following inputs:

Direct materials	3 kg @ £6.20 per kg
Direct labour	7 hours @ £8.00 per hour
Rent/rates	£24,000 per quarter
Leased delivery vans	£1,000 for every 900 units of production
Warehouse costs	£10,000 per quarter plus £2.00 per unit

Complete the table to show the total cost of production and the cost per unit at each of the quarterly production levels.

Production level - units	Total cost of production - £	Cost per unit £
2,000		
3,000		
4,000		

....

Task 1.3

A business produces a single product in its factory which has two production departments, cutting and finishing. In the following quarter it is anticipated that 200,000 units of the product will be produced. The expected costs are:

Direct materials	£10 per unit
Direct labour	3 hours cutting @ £8.00 per hour
	1 hour finishing @ £9.00 per hour
Variable overheads cutting	£444,000
finishing	£382,000
Fixed overheads cutting	£240,000
finishing	£110,000

Overheads are absorbed on the basis of direct labour hours.

(a) **The absorption cost per unit is**

    A   £45.65

    B   £46.60

    C   £47.13

    D   £48.88

(b) **The marginal cost per unit is**

    A   £45.65

    B   £46.60

    C   £47.13

    D   £48.88

....

Task 1.4

A company budgeted to produce 80,000 of its product with a standard cost of £4.60 per unit but in fact produced 84,000 units.

The actual costs of production were:

Materials	278,850
Packaging	8,800
Labour	17,100
Fixed overheads	85,000

The variances for the period have already been calculated:

Materials price	Zero	
Materials usage	£1,650	Adverse
Packaging price	£400	Adverse
Packaging usage	Zero	
Labour rate	£900	Favourable
Labour efficiency	£1,200	Adverse
Fixed overhead expenditure	£5,000	Adverse
Fixed overhead efficiency	£6,000	Adverse
Fixed overhead capacity	£10,000	Favourable

Calculate the budgeted cost for 84,000 units and then complete the table with the variances to reconcile to the actual cost of production.

Budgeted cost for actual production			
Variances	Favourable	Adverse	
Materials price			
Materials usage			
Packaging price			
Packaging usage			
Labour rate			
Labour efficiency			
Fixed overhead expenditure			
Fixed overhead efficiency			
Fixed overhead capacity			
Total variance			
Actual cost of actual production			

Task 1.5

You have been given an equation and information to estimate the cost of raw materials for the coming two months.

The equation is $Y = a + bX$, where

- X is the time period in months
- The value for X in May 20X8 is 25
- Y is the cost of raw materials
- the constant "**a**" is 125 and constant "**b**" is 2

The cost of raw materials is set on the first day of each month and is not changed during the month. The cost of the raw materials in May 20X8 was £175 per tonne.

(a) **Calculate the expected price of the raw material per tonne for June and July 20X8**

June cost per tonne (£)	
July cost per tonne (£)	

(b) **Convert the raw materials prices per tonne for June and July to index numbers using May 20X8 as the base (correct to two decimal places).**

June index	
July index	

··

Task 1.6

A company is developing a new product to monitor energy consumption. There are currently several other companies manufacturing similar products which sell for a price of £25 each. The company wishes to make a margin of 30%.

The target cost of each new product is £ [   ]

··

Task 1.7

The following information relates to one period for a single product produced by a company.

Expected sales revenue = £400,000

Selling price per unit = £40 per unit

Variable cost = £18 per unit

Fixed costs = £99,000

The breakeven point both in terms of units and sales revenue is:

	Breakeven point in units	Breakeven point in sales revenue
A	4,500 units	£99,000
B	4,500 units	£180,000
C	2,475 units	£99,000
D	2,475 units	£180,000

Task 1.8

(a) Given below are the production cost figures for the last nine months.

Calculate a three month moving average for these figures.

	Production costs	Three month moving total	Three month moving average
	£	£	£
March	226,500		
April	245,300		
May	240,800		
June	231,400		
July	237,600		
August	246,000		
September	241,200		
October	242,300		
November	247,500		
December	249,300		

(b) **The three month moving average represents which of the following?**

    A   Random variations

    B   Seasonal variations

    C   Trend

    D   Cyclical variations

Section 2

Task 2.1

Voltair Ltd has developed a domestic wind turbine. A colleague has prepared forecast information based upon two scenarios. The forecast income statements (profit and loss account) and statements of financial position (balance sheet) for both scenarios are shown below.

- Scenario 1 is to set the price at £1,250 per unit with sales of 10,000 units each year.
- Scenario 2 is to set the price at £1,000 per unit with sales of 14,000 units each year.

Forecast income statement

	Scenario 1	Scenario 2
	£'000	£'000
Revenue (turnover)	12,500	14,000
Cost of production:		
Direct (raw) materials	3,000	4,200
Direct labour	2,000	2,800
Fixed production overheads	3,000	3,000
Total cost of sales	8,000	10,000
Gross profit	4,500	4,000
Selling and distribution costs	1,000	1,000
Administration costs	750	750
Operating profit	2,750	2,250
Interest payable	600	600
Net profit	2,150	1,650

Extracts from the forecast statement of financial position

	£'000	£'000
Non-current (fixed) assets	20,000	20,000
Current assets	5,000	5,500
Current liabilities	4,600	5,800
Long-term loans	12,000	11,300
	8,400	8,400
Represented by:		
Share capital	5,650	6,150
Reserves	2,750	2,250
	8,400	8,400

(a) **Calculate the following performance indicators for each scenario:**

    (i)   gross profit margin

    (ii)   net profit margin

    (iii) direct materials cost per unit

    (iv) direct labour cost per unit

    (v)   fixed production cost per unit

    (vi) gearing ratio

    (vii) interest cover

(b) **Draft a report for the Finance Director covering the following:**

    (i)   an explanation of why the gross profit margin is different in each scenario. Your answer should refer to the following:

        –   sales price per unit

        –   materials, labour and fixed cost per unit

    (ii)   an assessment of the level of gearing and interest cover and whether it is a problem for the business

REPORT

To: Finance Director   **Subject:** Gross profit margin, gearing and interest cover

From: AAT Trainee   **Date:**   16 June 20X8

(i) **Gross profit margin**

(ii) **Gearing and interest cover**

Task 2.2

You are employed as an accounting technician at BeThere Airlines, a company that operates flights across Europe. The company has several divisions including a catering division operating from Manchester. The catering division produces meals daily for the flights. Currently all meals produced are used only on BeThere flights.

The company operates an integrated standard cost system in which:

- purchases of materials are recorded at standard cost
- direct material costs and direct labour costs are variable
- production overheads are fixed and absorbed using direct labour hours.

The budgeted activity and actual results for November 20X6 are as follows:

		Budget		Actual
Production (meals)		112,000		117,600
Direct materials	56,000 kgs	£224,000	61,740 kgs	£185,220
Direct labour	28,000 hours	£252,000	27,930 hours	£279,300
Fixed overheads		£84,000		£82,000
Total cost		£560,000		£546,520

(a) **Calculate the following information for November (to two decimal places):**

    (i)   standard price of materials per kilogram

    (ii)   standard usage of materials per meal

    (iii) standard labour rate per hour

    (iv) standard labour hours per meal

    (v)   budgeted overhead absorption rate per hour

    (vi) overheads absorbed into actual production

    (vii) the total standard cost of actual production

(b) **Calculate the following variances for November:**

    (i)   direct material price variance

    (ii)   direct material usage variance

    (iii) direct labour rate variance

    (iv) direct labour efficiency variance

    (v)   fixed overhead expenditure variance

    (vi) fixed overhead volume variance

    (vii) fixed overhead capacity variance

    (viii) fixed overhead efficiency variance

(c) Prepare a report to the managing director giving ONE possible reason for each of the following variances you calculated in (b).

    (i)   direct material price variance

    (ii)   direct material usage variance

    (iii) direct labour rate variance

    (iv) direct labour efficiency variance

REPORT

To: Managing Director

From: Accounting Technician

Subject: Reasons for the variances

Date: 14 December 20X6

Direct material price variance

Direct material usage variance

Direct labour rate variance

Direct labour efficiency variance

PRACTICE ASSESSMENT 2
FINANCIAL PERFORMANCE

ANSWERS

Section 1

Task 1.1

Standard cost card for 1,000 tea bags	
	£
Direct materials – tea (3kg × £5)	15.00
Direct materials – bags (1,000 × £0.006)	6.00
Direct labour $\left(\dfrac{1,000}{5,000 \text{ hours}} \times £10 \right)$	2.00
Fixed overhead $\left(\dfrac{0.2 \text{ hours} \times £200,000}{4,000 \text{ hours}} \right)$	10.00
Total standard cost	33.00

Task 1.2

Production level - units	Total cost of production - £	Cost per unit - £
2,000	190,200	95.10
3,000	267,800	89.27
4,000	345,400	86.35

Workings

	2,000 units £	3,000 units £	4,000 units £
Direct materials 3kgs x £6.20 x units	37,200	55,800	74,400
Direct labour 7 hours x £8.00 x units	112,000	168,000	224,000
Rent/rates	24,000	24,000	24,000
Leased delivery vans	3,000	4,000	5,000
Warehouse costs £10,000 + £2.00 x units	14,000	16,000	18,000
	190,200	267,800	345,400
Cost per unit	£95.10	£89.27	£86.35

Task 1.3

(a) D

(b) C

Workings

(a) **Absorption costing**

	£
Direct materials	10.00
Direct labour – cutting (3 × £8.00)	24.00
Finishing	9.00
Variable overheads:	
Cutting (£444,000/600,000) x 3 hrs	2.22
Finishing (£382,000/200,000) x 1hr	1.91
Fixed overheads:	
Cutting (£240,000/600,000) x 3 hrs	1.20
Finishing (£110,000/200,000) x 1 hr	<u>0.55</u>
	<u>48.88</u>

(b) **Marginal costing**

	£
Direct materials	10.00
Direct labour – Cutting (3 × £8.00)	24.00
Finishing	9.00
Variable overheads:	
Cutting (£440,000/600,000) x 3 hrs	2.22
Finishing (£382,000/200,000) x 1 hr	<u>1.91</u>
	<u>47.13</u>

Task 1.4

Operating statement

	£	£	£
Budgeted cost for actual production (84,000 x £4.60)			**386,400**
Variances	**Favourable**	**Adverse**	
Materials price	-	-	
Materials usage		1,650	
Packaging price		400	
Packaging usage	-	-	
Labour rate	900		
Labour efficiency		1,200	
Fixed overhead expenditure		5,000	
Fixed overhead efficiency		6,000	
Fixed overhead capacity	10,000		
Total variance	10,900	14,250	3,350
Actual cost of actual production (£278,850 + £8,800 + £17,100 + £85,000)			389,750

Task 1.5

(a)

June cost per tonne (£)	177
July cost per tonne (£)	179

Workings

$Y = a + bX$

For June, $X = 26$, therefore $Y = 125 + (2 \times 26) = £177$ per tonne

For July = $X = 27$, therefore $Y = 125 + (2 \times 27) = £179$ per tonne

(b)

June index	101.14
July index	102.29

Workings

As May is the base,   May = 100 when price was £175 per tonne

Therefore,   June = 177/175 x 100 = 101.14

                    July = 179/175 x 100 = 102.29

....

Task 1.6

Target cost = market price – desired profit margin

           = £25 – (£25 x 30%)

           = £25 – £7.50

           = £17.50

....

Task 1.7

B

Workings

Contribution per unit = £(40 – 18) = £22

Contribution required to breakeven = fixed costs = £99,000

Breakeven point = $\dfrac{\text{Fixed costs}}{\text{Contribution per unit}}$

                = $\dfrac{£99,000}{£22}$

                = 4,500 units

Sales revenue at breakeven point = 4,500 units × £40 per unit

                                  = £180,000

....

Task 1.8

(a)

	Production costs	Three month moving total	Three month moving average
	£	£	£
March	226,500		
April	245,300	712,600	237,533
May	240,800	717,500	239,167
June	231,400	709,800	236,600
July	237,600	715,000	238,333
August	246,000	724,800	241,600
September	241,200	729,500	243,167
October	242,300	731,000	243,667
November	247,500	739,100	246,367
December	249,300		

(b)   C   Trend

Section 2

Task 2.1

(a)

	Scenario 1	Scenario 2
(i) Gross profit margin		
= Gross Profit / Revenue (turnover) x 100	(4,500 / 12,500) x 100 = 36.00%	(4,000 / 14,000) x 100 = 28.57%
(ii) Net profit margin		
= Net Profit / Revenue x 100	(2,150 / 12,500) x 100 = 17.20%	(1,650 / 14,000) x 100 = 11.79%
(iii) Direct materials cost per unit		
= Direct materials cost / sales units	£3,000,000 / 10,000 = £300	£4,200,000 / 14,000 = £300
(iv) Direct labour cost per unit		
= Direct labour cost / sales units	£2,000,000 / 10,000 = £200	£2,800,000 / 14,000 = £200
(v) Fixed production cost per unit		
= Fixed production cost / sales units	£3,000,000 / 10,000 = £300	£3,000,000 / 14,000 = £214.29

(vi) Gearing

= Long term loans/ (long term loans + share capital + reserves)	12,000 / (12,000 + 8,400)= (0.5882 or 58.82%)	11,300/(11,300+8,400)= 0.5736 or 57.36%

Alternative answer for gearing:

Gearing

= Long term loans/ (share capital + reserves)	12,000/8,400 =	11,300/8,400 =
	(1.4286 or 142.86%)	(1.3452 or 134.52%)

(vii) Interest cover

= Operating profit / interest payable	2,750/600 = 4.58	2,250/600 = 3.75

(b)

REPORT

To: Finance Director **Subject:** Gross profit margin, gearing and interest cover

From: AAT Trainee **Date:** 16 June 20X8

(i) **Gross profit margin**

The gross profit margin for scenario 1 is 36% and scenario 2 is 28.57%. Direct materials and labour are the same under both scenarios so that the higher gross profit margin for scenario 1 must be as a result of differences in sales price per unit or fixed production overheads. In fact the fixed costs per unit are higher under scenario 1 because less volume is produced (£300 per unit as opposed to £214.29 per unit for scenario 2). Therefore the reason for the higher gross margin is the higher price per unit (£1,250 and £1,000 respectively).

(ii) **Gearing and interest cover**

The level of gearing for both scenarios is at a similar level and there appears to be reasonable security in the form of non-current (fixed) assets. Everything else being equal the higher the gearing ratio the higher the risk. This is because long term loans has interest payments that have to be made from operating profit. However, the gearing indicator cannot be considered in isolation. Voltair's ability to service the debt is also important.

The level of interest cover shows how many times Voltair can pay its interest payable out of operating profit. For scenario 1 the profit is 4.58 times greater than interest payable. This falls slightly to 3.75 times for scenario 2 due to the fall in profits, as the interest payable is constant under both scenarios.

Both scenarios have a relatively high interest cover and this does not appear to be a problem for the business.

Task 2.2

(a) (i) Standard price of materials per kg $= \dfrac{\text{Budgeted total materials cost}}{\text{Budgeted total materials usage in kg}}$

$$= \frac{£224,000}{56,000}$$

$$= £4 \text{ per kg}$$

(ii) Standard usage of materials per meal $= \dfrac{\text{Budgeted total materials usage in kg}}{\text{Production (meals)}}$

$$= \frac{56,000}{112,000}$$

$$= 0.5 \text{ kg}$$

(iii) Standard labour rate per hour $= \dfrac{\text{Budgeted total labour cost}}{\text{Budgeted total labour hours}}$

$$= \frac{£252,000}{28,000}$$

$$= £9 \text{ per hour}$$

(iv) Standard labour hours per meal $= \dfrac{\text{Budgeted total labour hours}}{\text{Production (meals)}}$

$$= \frac{28,000}{112,000}$$

$$= 0.25 \text{ hours (or 15 minutes)}$$

(v) Budgeted overhead absorption rate per hour $= \dfrac{\text{Budgeted total overhead cost}}{\text{Budgeted total labour hours}}$

$$= \frac{£84,000}{28,000}$$

$$= £3 \text{ per hour}$$

(vi) Overheads absorbed into actual production $= 27,930 \text{ hours} \times £3$

$$= £83,790$$

(vii) Total standard cost of actual production $= £560,000 \times \dfrac{117,600}{112,000}$

$$= £588,000$$

Alternatively:

	Standard cost per meal
	£
Direct material (0.5 kg × £4)	2.00
Direct labour (0.25 hours × £9)	2.25
Fixed overheads (0.25 hours × £3)	0.75
	5.00

Total standard cost of actual production = 117,600 meals × £5 per meal

= £588,000

(b) Variance calculations:

		£	£
(i)	**Direct material price variance**		
	Actual materials at actual cost	185,220	
	Actual materials at standard cost (61,740kg × £4)	246,960	
			61,740 (F)
(ii)	**Direct material usage variance**		
	Actual materials at standard cost (61,740kg × £4)	246,960	
	Standard materials for actual production at standard cost (117,600 × 0.5kg × £4)	235,200	
			11,760 (A)
(iii)	**Direct labour rate variance**		
	Actual hours at actual rate	279,300	
	Actual hours at standard rate (27,930 × £9)	251,370	
			27,930 (A)
(iv)	**Direct labour efficiency variance**		
	Actual hours at standard rate (27,930 × £9)	251,370	
	Standard hours for actual production at standard rate (117,600 × 0.25 hours × £9)	264,600	
			13,230 (F)
(v)	**Fixed overhead expenditure variance**		
	Actual cost	82,000	
	Budgeted cost	84,000	
			2,000 (F)

(vi) **Fixed overhead volume variance**

Actual production volume at standard rate		
(117,600 × 0.25 × £3)	88,200	
Budgeted production volume at standard rate		
(112,000 × 0.25 × £3)	84,000	4,200 (F)

Tutorial note: This is a favourable variance because a greater production volume has been achieved than was budgeted for. The two variances below are a further analysis of the volume variance and the sum of the two will therefore equal the volume variance. The capacity variance looks at how the actual production hours differs from the originally budgeted hours. The efficiency variance compares actual with the flexed budget, and is the same type of calculation as the labour efficiency variance.

	£	£
(vii) **Fixed overhead capacity variance**		
Budgeted hours at standard rate (28,000 × £3)	84,000	
Actual hours at standard rate (27,930 × £3)	83,790	
		210 (A)
(viii) **Fixed overhead efficiency variance**		
Actual hours at standard rate (27,930 × £3)	83,790	
Standard hours for actual production at		
standard rate (117,600 × 0.25 × £3)	88,200	
		4,410 (F)

(c)

REPORT

To: Managing Director

From: Accounting Technician

Subject: Reasons for the variances

Date: 14 December 20X6

Having investigated the materials and labour variances calculated for November 20X6, I can suggest the following possible causes.

(i)   Direct materials price variance £61,740 (F)

This variance resulted from the purchase of materials at £3 per kg rather than the standard cost of £4 per kg. This material was cheaper and possibly of a lower quality.

(ii) Direct material usage variance £11,760 (A)

The actual usage was worse than expected, and this could have been a consequence of buying inferior material.

(iii) Direct labour rate variance £27,930 (A)

Direct workers were actually paid at £10 per hour, whilst we had only budgeted for a rate of £9 per hour. It is possible that the workers used were more skilled than we planned for.

(iv) Direct labour efficiency variance £13,230 (F)

Actual production required fewer hours than were expected which is consistent with using more highly-skilled staff.

Tutorial note: There is more than one possible reason for each of the above variances, and marks would have been awarded for any reasonable suggestions.

....

PRACTICE ASSESSMENT 3
FINANCIAL PERFORMANCE

Time allowed: 2.5 hours

Section 1

Task 1.1

(a) A company purchases 14,000 kgs of material at a cost of £58,000. The standard cost per Kg is £4.

The total materials price variance is

A £14,000

B £2,000

C £58,000

D £4.14

(b) A company purchases 10,000 kgs of material at a cost of £22,000. The budgeted production was 6,000 units which requires 9,000 kgs of material at a total standard cost of £18,000. The actual production was 6,500 units.

The material usage variance is

A 500 kgs

B 250 kgs

C £500

D £250

(c) A company's product is budgeted to require 3 hours of labour at £9 per hour. The budgeted production level was 12,000 units but actual production was 11,400 units. the actual hours worked were 33,600 at a cost of £320,400.

The labour rate variance is

A £18,000

B 2,000 hours

C £0.54

D £1,800

. . . .

Task 1.2

The budgeted activity and actual results for a business for the month of May 20X8 are as follows:

		Budget		Actual
Production (tonnes)		200		210
Direct labour	600 hours	£4,800	600 hours	£5,100
Fixed overheads		£90,000		£95,000

(a) **Complete the table to calculate the following:**

	£
Budgeted overhead absorption rate per tonne	
Overheads absorbed into actual production	
Fixed overhead expenditure variance	
Fixed overhead volume variance	

Task 1.3

A material which is derived from soft fruit is either imported or purchased from UK farmers by a company. The price of the material fluctuates month by month depending on the time of year. The cost information for the 4 months ending August 20X6 is given below.

	May X6	June X6	July X6	August X6
Cost per 1,000 kg	£1,000	£900	£700	£800

The underlying cost does not change during the period May to August. The change in cost over the 4 months is due only to the seasonal variations which are given below.

	May X6	June X6	July X6	August X6
Seasonal variations	£200	£100	-£100	£0

(a) **Complete the table to calculate the underlying cost per 1,000 kilograms for the period May to August 20X6.**

	May 20X6 £	June 20X6 £	July 20X6 £	Aug 20X6 £
Cost per 1,000 kgs				
Seasonal variation				
Trend				

(b) Indications are that the underlying cost per 1,000 kilograms for the period May 20X7 to August 20X7 will be £850.

The percentage increase in the underlying cost from 20X6 to 20X7 is [   ] **%**

(c) **Complete the table to calculate the forecast cost per 1,000 kilograms for the period May 20X7 to August 20X7 using the underlying cost and the seasonal variations given above.**

	May 20X7	June 20X7	July 20X7	Aug 20X7
	£	£	£	£
Trend				
Seasonal variation				
Cost per 1,000 kgs				

Task 1.4

You have been given an equation and information to estimate aviation fuel costs for an airline company for the coming three months.

The equation is $Y = a + bX$ where:

- X is the time period in months

- Y is the cost of aviation fuel

- the value for X in November 20X6 is 11

- the constant 'a' is 0.998 and the constant 'b' is 0.002.

The cost of aviation fuel is set on the first day of each month and is not changed during the month. The cost of fuel in November 20X6 was £1.020 per litre.

Complete the table to calculate the expected price of fuel for December 20X6, and January and February 20X7.

	£
December 20X6	
January 20X7	
February 20X7	

Task 1.5

Voltair Ltd has developed a domestic wind turbine. A colleague has prepared forecast information based upon two scenarios. The forecast income statement (profit and loss account) for both scenarios is shown below.

- Scenario 1 is to set the price at £1,250 per unit with sales of 10,000 units each year.

- Scenario 2 is to set the price at £1,000 per unit with sales of 14,000 units each year.

Forecast income statement		
	Scenario 1	Scenario 2
	£'000	£'000
Revenue (turnover)	12,500	14,000
Cost of production		
Direct (raw) materials	3,000	4,200
Direct labour	2,000	2,800
Fixed production overheads	3,000	3,000
Cost of sales	8,000	10,000
Gross profit	4,500	4,000
Selling and distribution costs	1,000	1,000
Administration costs	750	750
Operating profit	2,750	2,250
Interest payable	600	600
Net profit	2,150	1,650

The Managing Director has been in talks with a Romanian manufacturer who could produce the wind turbines. You have been asked to analyse the information in order to evaluate whether Voltair should contract out the manufacture of the turbines.

If the turbines are manufactured in Romania the costs and savings would be as follows:

- The cost of each turbine would be £650 including transport costs to the UK.

- The material and labour costs would be saved.

- The fixed production costs consist of £1.95 million of specific costs which would be avoided, and £1.05 million of allocated overheads which would not be avoided.

(a) **Complete the table to calculate the following information for the demand level of 10,000 turbines per annum:**

	£
Full production cost per turbine manufactured by Voltair	
Voltair's unavoidable fixed production cost per turbine if contracted out	
Voltair's avoidable production cost per turbine if contracted out	

(b) **Complete the table to calculate the following information for the demand level of 14,000 turbines per annum:**

	£
Full production cost per turbine manufactured by Voltair	
Voltair's unavoidable fixed production cost per turbine if contracted out	
Voltair's avoidable production cost per turbine if contracted out	

Task 1.6

A company is reviewing various alternatives to determine whether it is possible to reduce monthly costs. The operations director is considering whether to invest in a new machine which:

- could either be purchased for £3 million or rented for £50,000 per month
- is expected to have a life of 10 years and a scrap value of £900,000.

It is assumed under both options that:

- the maintenance cost of the machine is £50,000 per annum
- decommissioning costs will be £100,000
- the machine will be used for 10 years

Calculate the lifecycle cost of the TWO options outlined

Ignore the time value of money and any opportunity costs when calculating the lifecycle cost.

Task 1.7

The costs of the maintenance department of a manufacturing business are estimated to be £102,000 for the following quarter. During that period it is estimated that there will be 50 maintenance visits on site. Product X will require 10 maintenance visits during the quarter and Product Y 40 maintenance visits.

Complete the table below using activity based costing to show how much maintenance overhead will be absorbed into Product X and Product Y.

	£
Overhead included in Product X	
Overhead included in Product Y	

Task 1.8

The standard direct materials cost for a business's product is:

14.4 kg @ £5.00 per kg = £72.00

During the month of May production was 9,200 units of the product and the actual materials cost was £671,600 for 135,500 kgs. The price of the materials has been unexpectedly increased to £5.70 per kg for the whole month.

The total materials price variance is £ [   ]

The planning element of the materials price variance that has been caused by the price increase is £ [   ]

The control element of the materials price variance caused by other factors is £ [   ]

....

Section 2

Task 2.1

A division of Fooddrink Ltd is developing a new supplement and a colleague has prepared forecast information based upon two scenarios. The forecast income statements (profit and loss accounts) and statements of financial position (balance sheets) for both scenarios are shown below.

- Scenario 1 is to set the price at £10 per unit with sales of 120,000 units each year.

- Scenario 2 is to set the price at £5 per unit with sales of 360,000 units each year.

	Scenario 1	Scenario 2
	£'000	£'000
Budgeted income statement		
Revenue (turnover)	1,200	1,800
Cost of production		
Direct (raw) materials	300	900
Direct labour	120	360
Fixed production overheads	360	360
Total cost of sales	780	1,620
Gross profit	420	180
Selling and distribution costs	74	122
Administration costs	100	100
Operating profit	246	(42)
Budgeted statement of financial position		
Non-current (fixed) assets		
Machinery	1,600	1,600
Current assets		
Inventory (stock) of raw materials	50	50
Receivables (debtors)	150	150
Current liabilities		
Payables (creditors)	75	75
Net current assets	125	125
Long-term loans	754	1,042
Net assets	971	683
Represented by:		
Share capital	725	725
Operating profit for the year	246	(42)
Share capital and reserves	971	683

(a) **Calculate the following performance indicators for both scenarios:**

    (i)   gross profit margin

    (ii)   operating profit margin

    (iii) direct materials as a percentage of revenue

    (iv) direct materials cost per unit

    (v)   return on net assets

    (vi) inventory turnover in days

    (vii) receivables' collectable period in days

    (viii) gearing

(b) **Draft a report for the finance director giving an explanation of why the following ratios have changed:**

    (i)   gross profit margin

    (ii)   operating profit margin

    (iii) direct materials as a percentage of revenue

To: Finance Director

Subject: Differences in key performance indicators

From: Accounting Technician

Date: 18 June 20X7

Gross profit margin

Operating profit margin

Direct materials

You have found that your colleague has made a few mistakes with the figures for Scenario 2. The income statement and statement of financial position amendments for Scenario 2 are listed below.

- The raw material price per unit will fall to £1.50 per unit.

- The closing inventory of raw materials will be £90,000.

- Receivables will be £225,000.

- Payables will be £45,000.

- Short-term borrowing will be £145,000.

- Long-term loans will be £682,000.

(c) **Recalculate the following information:**

    (i)   gross profit

    (ii) operating profit

    (iii) net assets

(d) **Recalculate the following ratios:**

    (i)   gross profit margin

    (ii) operating profit margin

    (iii) return on net assets

(e) **Redraft your report for the finance director commenting on the ratios you recalculated in (d) above and recommend whether the price of the product should be set at £10 or £5.**

To: Financial Director

Subject: Differences in key performance indicators

From: Accounting Technician

Date: 18 June 20X7

Gross profit margin

Operating profit margin

Return on net assets

Recommendations

· ·

Task 2.2

Croxton Ltd makes a specialised chemical, X14, in barrels at its factory. The factory has two departments: the processing department and the finishing department. Because of the technology involved, Croxton apportions both budgeted and actual total factory fixed overheads between the two departments on the basis of budgeted machine hours.

The standard absorption cost per barrel of X14 in the processing department, and the budgeted production for the five weeks ended 31 May 20X8, are shown below.

Processing department: standard cost per barrel of X14			
Input	**Quantity**	**Standard price/rate**	**Cost**
			£
Material	10 litres	£60 per litre	600
Labour	8 labour hrs	£8 per labour hr	64
Fixed overheads	16 machine hrs	£20 per machine hr	320
Standard absorption cost per barrel			984
Budgeted production 5 weeks ending 31 May 20X8			45 barrels

You are employed by Croxton Ltd as an accounting technician. One of your duties is to prepare standard costing reconciliation statements. Croxton's finance director gives you the following information for the five weeks ended 31 May 20X8.

Total factory budgeted and actual data

- Factory budgeted machine hours   1,152 machine hours
- Factory budgeted fixed overheads   £23,040
- Factory actual fixed overheads   £26,000
- Budgeted **and** actual factory fixed overheads are apportioned between the processing and finishing departments **on the basis of budgeted machine hours**.

Processing department actual data

- Actual costs

  Materials at £58.50 per litre   £23,985

  Labour (328 hours)   £2,788

- Actual production output   40 barrels
- Actual machine hours worked   656 hours
- There was no work in progress at any stage.

(a) **Calculate the following information for the processing department.**

   (i)   Actual litres of material used

   (ii)   Standard litres of material required for 40 barrels of X14

   (iii) Average actual labour rate per hour

   (iv) Standard labour hours required for 40 barrels of X14

   (v)   Budgeted number of machine hours

   (vi) Budgeted fixed overheads

   (vii) Actual fixed overheads (based on its share of actual factory overhead)

   (viii) Standard machine hours for actual production

      (ix) Standard absorption cost of actual production

      (x) Actual absorption cost of actual production

(b) **Using data given and your answers to part (a), calculate the following variances for the processing department.**

      (i)   Material price variance

      (ii)   Material usage variance

      (iii) Labour rate variance

      (iv) Labour efficiency variance

      (v)   Fixed overhead expenditure variance

      (vi) Fixed overhead volume variance

      (vii) Fixed overhead efficiency variance

      (viii) Fixed overhead capacity variance

(c) **Prepare a statement for the five weeks ended 31 May 20X8 reconciling the standard absorption cost of actual production with the actual absorption cost of actual production.**

Reconciliation statement – five weeks ended 31 May 20X8			
			£
Standard absorption cost of actual production			
	£	£	
	(F)	(A)	
Variances			
Material price			
Material usage			
Labour rate			
Labour efficiency			
Fixed overhead expenditure			
Fixed overhead efficiency			
Fixed overhead capacity			
Actual absorption cost of actual production			

(d) Judith Green is the production manager of the processing department. You show her the statement reconciling the actual and standard costs of actual production. Judith then gives you the following additional information.

- When the standard costs were agreed, a price index for the material used in making the X14 was 140, but during the five weeks ended 31 May it was 133.

- Actual production output was 40 barrels but Croxton had to make 41 barrels of X14 as one barrel had to be scrapped on completion. This was because the barrel was damaged. The scrapped barrel had no value.

- If labour hours worked exceed 320 hours per five weeks, overtime is incurred. The overtime premium is £8.00 per hour of overtime.

- There is just one customer for the X14. The customer purchased 40 barrels during the five weeks ended 31 May 20X8.

Judith believes there is no need to examine the variances any further, for a number of reasons.

- The material price variance clearly shows that the purchasing department is efficient.

- The labour rate, labour efficiency and material usage variances were entirely due to the one scrapped barrel.

- Fixed overheads are not controllable by the processing department.

Write a memo to Judith Green. In your memo you should do the following.

(i) Use the material price index to identify a revised standard price for the materials used in X14.

(ii) Subdivide the material price variance calculated in task (b) (i) into that part due to the change in the price index and that part due to other reasons.

(iii) Briefly explain whether the material price variance calculated in task (b) (i) arose from efficiencies in the purchasing department.

(iv) Explain whether the one scrapped barrel might fully account for the following.

    (1) Material usage variance

    (2) Labour efficiency variance

    (3) Labour rate variance

(v) Give ONE reason why the fixed overheads might not be controllable by the processing department.

MEMO

To: Judith Green, production manager

From: Accounting technician

Date: 7 August 20X5

Subject: **Croxton Ltd – analysis of variances for 5 weeks ended 31 May 20X8**

PRACTICE ASSESSMENT 3
FINANCIAL PERFORMANCE

ANSWERS

Section 1

Task 1.1

(a) B

		£
Standard cost	14,000 x £4	56,000
Actual cost		58,000
Total materials price variance		2,000

(b) C

	£
Standard usage 6,500 x 1.5 kgs @ standard cost £2	19,500
Actual usage 10,000 kgs @ standard cost £2	20,000
Materials usage variance	500

(c) A

	£
Actual hours at standard cost 33,600 x £9	302,400
Actual hours at actual cost	320,400
Labour rate variance	18,000

Task 1.2

Budgeted overhead absorption rate per tonne	£450
Overheads absorbed into actual production	£94,500
Fixed overhead expenditure variance	£5,000 Adverse
Fixed overhead volume variance	£4,500 Favourable

Workings

budgeted overhead absorption rate per tonne	= fixed overheads / budgeted output
	= £90,000 / 200 tonnes
	= £450
overheads absorbed into actual production	= actual production x absorption rate
	= 210 units x £450
	= £94,500

Fixed overhead expenditure variance

	£
Budgeted fixed overhead	90,000
Actual fixed overhead	95,000
Fixed overhead expenditure variance	5,000 Adv

Fixed overhead volume variance

	£
Actual production at absorption rate per unit (210 x £450)	94,500
Budgeted production at absorption rate per unit	90,000
Fixed overhead volume variance	4,500 Fav

....

Task 1.3

(a)

	May 20X6	June 20X6	July 20X6	Aug 20X6
	£	£	£	£
Cost per 1,000 kgs	1,000	900	700	800
Seasonal variation	200	100	(100)	0
Trend	800	800	800	800

Tutorial note. The underlying cost is the Trend.

(b) The percentage increase in the underlying cost from 20X6 to 20X7 is 6.25%

$$\left(\frac{(850 - 800)}{800} \right) \times 100 = 6.25\%$$

Tutorial note. The above calculation is the most normal way of calculating a change from one period to the next, as a percentage of the original figure.

(c)

	May 20X7	June 20X7	July 20X7	Aug 20X7
	£	£	£	£
Trend	850	850	850	850
Seasonal variation	200	100	(100)	0
Cost per 1,000 kgs	1,050	950	750	850

Task 1.4

	£
December 20X6	£1.022
January 20X7	£1.024
February 20X7	£1.026

Workings

December 20X6	=	0.998 + 0.002 × 12	=	£1.022 per litre
January 20X7	=	0.998 + 0.002 × 13	=	£1.024 per litre
February 20X7	=	0.998 + 0.002 × 14	=	£1.026 per litre

Task 1.5

(a)

Full production cost per turbine manufactured by Voltair	£800.00
Voltair's unavoidable fixed production cost per turbine if contracted out	£105.00
Voltair's avoidable production cost per turbine if contracted out	£695.00

(b)

Full production cost per turbine manufactured by Voltair	£714.29
Voltiar's unavoidable fixed production cost per turbine if contracted out	£75.00
Voltaire's avoidable production cost per turbine if contracted out	£639.29

Workings

(a) (i) Full production cost per turbine based upon production of 10,000 turbines = £8,000,000

Therefore cost per turbine = £8,000,000 / 10,000 = £800.00

(ii) Unavoidable fixed production cost = £3,000,000 - £1,950,000 = £1,050,000

Therefore unavoidable fixed production cost per turbine for 10,000 units = £1,050,000 / 10,000 = £105.00

(iii) Avoidable production cost per turbine for 10,000 units = £800 - £105 = £695.00

(b) (i) Full production cost per turbine based upon production of 14,000 turbines = £10,000,000

Therefore cost per turbine = £10,000,000 / 14,000 = £714.29

(ii) Unavoidable fixed production cost = £3,000,000 - £1,950,000 = £1,050,000

Therefore unavoidable fixed production cost per turbine for 14,000 units = £1,050,000 / 14,000 = £75.00

(iii) Avoidable production cost per turbine for 14000 units = £714.29 - £75.00 = £639.29

....

Task 1.6

Lifecycle costs of renting the machine:

	£
Rental (£50,000 × 12 months × 10 years)	6,000,000
Maintenance (£50,000 × 10 years)	500,000
Decommissioning	100,000
Total	6,600,000

Lifecycle costs of buying the machine:

	£
Purchase	3,000,000
Maintenance (£50,000 × 10 years)	500,000
Decommissioning	100,000
Scrap value	(900,000)
Total	2,700,000

....

Task 1.7

Overhead included in Product X	£20,400
Overhead included in Product Y	£81,600

Workings

Maintenance cost per visit   =   £102,000/50   =   £2,040

Product X   =   10 x £2,040   =   £20,400

Product Y   =   40 x £2,040   =   £81,600

....

Task 1.8

The total materials price variance is £5,900

The planning element of the materials price variance that has been caused by the price increase is £94,850

The control element of the materials price variance caused by other factors is £100,750

Workings

Total materials price variance

	£
Standard cost for actual quantity 135,500 x £5	677,500
Actual cost	671,600
	5,900 (F)

Planning variance caused by price increase

	£
Standard cost for actual quantity 135,500 x £5.00	677,500
Adjusted cost for actual quantity 135,500 x £5.70	772,350
	94,850 (A)

Control variance caused by other factors

	£
Adjusted cost for actual quantity 135,500 x £5.70	772,350
Actual cost	671,600
	100,750 (F)

....

Section 2

Task 2.1

(a) **Tutorial note.** The workings are shown for scenario 1 – the workings for scenario 2 are similar.

	Scenario 1	Scenario 2
Gross profit margin £ $\left(\dfrac{420,000}{1,200,000}\right) \times 100$	35.00%	10.00%
Operating profit margin £ $\left(\dfrac{246,000}{1,200,000}\right) \times 100$	20.50%	−2.33% or 0
Direct materials as a percentage of revenue		
£$\left(\dfrac{300,000}{1,200,000}\right) \times 100$	25.00%	50.00%
Direct materials cost per unit £ $\left(\dfrac{300,000}{120,000}\right)$	£2.50	£2.50
Return on net assets $\left(\dfrac{246,000}{971,000}\right) \times 100$	25.33%	−6.15% or 0
Inventory turnover in days (based on raw materials)		
$\left(\dfrac{50,000}{300,000}\right) \times 365$ or	60.83 days	20.28 days
Inventory turnover in days (based on total cost of sales)		
$\left(\dfrac{50,000}{780,000}\right) \times 365$	23.40 days	11.27 days
Receivables' colllectable period in days		
$\left(\dfrac{150,000}{1,200,000}\right) \times 365$	45.63 days	30.42 days
Gearing (long term loans/(long term loans + share capital + reserves)		
$\left(\dfrac{754,000}{(754,000 + 971,000)}\right) \times 100$	43.71%	60.41%
Gearing (long term loans/(share capital + reserves) $\left(\dfrac{754,000}{971,000}\right) \times 100$	77.65% or 0.78:1	152.56% or 1.53:1

(b) **To:** Finance Director

Subject: Differences in key performance indicators

From: Accounting Technician

Date: 18 June 20X7

(i) **Gross profit margin**

The gross profit margin for scenario 1 is 35% but falls to 10% for scenario 2. There are two causes for this difference. The selling price has been reduced by 50% (from £10 to £5) which will have reduced the margin. The reduction in the selling price has however increased the volume produced and sold which has reduced the fixed overhead per unit which will have increased the margin. However, the effect of the decreased selling price in reducing the margin has outweighed the beneficial effect of the fixed overheads.

(ii) **Operating profit margin**

The operating profit margin for scenario 1 is 20.5%, this falls to a loss under scenario 2. The reduction in gross profit margin has fed down to the operating profit margin and the selling and distribution costs have increased due to the higher sales volume.

(iii) **Direct materials**

The direct materials cost as a percentage of turnover has increased from 25% under scenario 1 to 50% under scenario 2. This fall is caused by the 50% reduction in the selling price. Every unit that is sold under the two scenarios has the same direct material cost (£2.50) but the selling price in scenario 2 is only £5 giving a percentage material cost of 50%, whereas the selling price in scenario 1 is £10 giving a percentage material cost of 25%.

(c)

	£
Gross profit	
Scenario 2 gross profit	180,000
Add back raw materials costs at £2.5 per unit (£2.5 x 360,000)	900,000
Less raw materials costs at £1.5 per unit for 360,000 units	(540,000)
Recalculated gross profit	540,000
Operating profit	
Recalculated gross profit	540,000
Less selling and distribution and administration costs (£122,000 + £100,000)	(222,000)
Recalculated operating profit	318,000
Net assets	
Share capital	725,000
Recalculated operating profit for the year	318,000
Revised net assets	1,043,000

or

	£
Net assets under Scenario 2	683,000
Increase in inventory of raw materials £(90,000 – 50,000)	40,000
Increase in receivables £(225,000 – 150,000)	75,000
Increase in short-term borrowing £(0 – 145,000)	(145,000)
Decrease in long-term loans £(1,042,000 – 682,000)	360,000
Decrease in payables £(75,000 – 45,000)	30,000
	1,043,000

(d)

	%
Gross profit margin £ $\left(\dfrac{540,000}{1,800,000}\right) \times 100$	30.00
Operating profit margin £ $\left(\dfrac{318,000}{1,800,000}\right) \times 100$	17.67
Return on net assets £ $\left(\dfrac{318,000}{1,043,000}\right) \times 100$	30.49

(e) **To:**   Financial Director

Subject: Differences in key performance indicators

From: Accounting Technician

Date: 18 June 20X7

(i) **Gross profit margin**

The revised gross profit has increased to 30%. The increase in the gross profit is caused by the reduction in the cost of raw materials per unit.

However, although the reduction in cost per unit increases the gross profit of scenario 2, it is still below the gross profit of scenario 1 because the effect of scenario 2's lower selling price outweighs the advantages of its lower raw materials and fixed cost absorption rate.

(ii) **Operating profit margin**

The revised operating profit for scenario 2 has increased to £318,000 from a loss. The operating profit margin is now improved to 18% which is fed through from the gross margin but this is still less than the 20.5% for scenario 1.

(iii) **Return on net assets**

The revised return on net assets for scenario 2 is 30.5% compared to 25% for scenario 1.

Recommendations

Based purely on the above three indicators, the decision should be to set the price at £5 as per scenario 2 because the higher return on net assets indicates that the return on investment is (pound for pound) better in scenario 2 and therefore will increase shareholder value. The fact that scenario 1 still has better gross and operating margins is not decisive. These margins do indicate that there are better operating efficiencies in scenario 1 compared to scenario 2. However, the fact that the revised figures for scenario 2 show that it has a significantly larger operating profit than scenario 1 with net assets for the two scenarios being almost the same causes the return on investment in scenario 2 to be better.

Task 2.2

(a) (i) **Actual litres of material used** = actual total cost of materials/actual cost per litre = £23,985/£58.50 = 410 litres

(ii) **Standard litres of material required for 40 barrels of X14** = standard litres per barrel × 40 = 10 litres × 40 = 400 litres

(iii) **Average actual labour rate per hour** = actual total cost of labour/actual number of hours = £2,788/328 hours = £8.50

(iv) **Standard labour hours required for 40 barrels of X14** = standard labour hours per barrel × 40 = 8 hours × 40 = 320 hours

(v) **Budgeted number of machine hours** = budgeted production × budgeted number of hours per barrel = 45 barrels × 16 = 720 hours

(vi) **Budgeted fixed overheads** = standard fixed overhead per barrel × budgeted production = £320 × 45 = £14,400

or = budgeted number of machine hours for processing department × standard rate per machine hour = 720 hours × £20 = £14,400

or = (budgeted machine hours for processing department/factory budgeted machine hours) × factory budgeted fixed overheads = (720 hours/1,152 hours) × £23,040 = £14,400)

(vii) **Actual fixed overheads** (for the processing department) = (budgeted machine hours for processing department/factory budgeted machine hours) × factory actual fixed overheads = (720 hours/1,152 hours) × £26,000 = £16,250

(viii) **Standard machine hours for actual production** = actual production output × standard machine hours per barrel = 40 barrels × 16 machine hours = 640 standard machine hours

(ix) **Standard absorption cost of actual production** = standard absorption cost per barrel × actual production = £984 × 40 barrels = £39,360

(x) **Actual absorption cost of actual production** = actual cost of material + labour + fixed overheads = £(23,985 + 2,788 + 16,250(a)(vii)) = £43,023

(b) (i) **Material price variance**

		£	
410 litres (from (a)(i)) should have cost (× £60)		24,600	
but did cost		23,985	
		615	(F)

(ii) **Material usage variance**

40 barrels should have used (× 10 litres) (from (a)(ii))	400	litres
but did use (from (a)(i))	410	litres
Variance in litres	10	litres (A)
× standard cost per litre	× £60	
	£600	(A)

(iii) **Labour rate variance**

	£	
328 hours should have cost (× £8)	2,624	
but did cost	2,788	
	164	(A)

(iv) **Labour efficiency variance**

40 barrels should have taken (× 8 hours) (from (a)(iv))	320	hours
but did take	328	hours
Variance in hours	8	hours (A)
× standard cost per hour	× £8	
	£64	(A)

(v) **Fixed overhead expenditure variance**

	£	
Budgeted fixed overhead expenditure (from (a)(vi))	14,400	
Actual fixed overhead expenditure (from (a)(vii))	16,250	
	1,850	(A)

(vi) **Fixed overhead volume variance**

	£	
Actual production at standard rate (40 barrels × £320)	12,800	
Budgeted production at standard rate (45 barrels × £320)	14,400	
	1,600	(A)

(vii) **Fixed overhead efficiency variance**

40 barrels should take (× 16 hours) (from (a)(viii))	640	hours
but did take	656	hours
Variance in hours	16	hours (A)
× standard rate per hour	× £20	
	£320	(A)

(viii) **Fixed overhead capacity variance**

Budgeted machine hours (from (a)(v))	720	
Actual machine hours	656	
Variance in hours	64	(A)
× standard absorption rate per hour	× £20	
	£1,280	(A)

(c) **Reconciliation statement – five weeks ended 31 May 20X8**

			£	
Standard absorption cost of actual production (from (a)(ix))			39,360	
	£	£		
	(F)	(A)		
Variances				
Material price	615			
Material usage		600		
Labour rate		164		
Labour efficiency		64		
Fixed overhead expenditure		1,850		
Fixed overhead efficiency		320		
Fixed overhead capacity		1,280		
	615	4,278	3,663	(A)
Actual absorption cost of actual production (from (a)(x))			43,023	

(d) **MEMO**

To: Judith Green, production manager

From: Accounting technician

Date: 7 August 20X5

Subject: **Croxton Ltd – analysis of variances for 5 weeks ended 31 May 20X8**

Following our recent meeting, I set out below some issues to consider in relation to our discussions.

(i)   **Revised standard material price per litre** = £60 x 133/140 = £57

(ii) **Subdivision of material price variance**

	£	£
410 litres were expected to have cost (at the original standard of £60 per litre)	24,600	
but should then have been expected to have cost (at the revised standard of £57 per litre)	23,370	
Variance due to the change in the price index		1,230 (F)
410 litres should have cost, if the revised standard of £57 had been used	23,370	
but did cost	23,985	
Variance due to other reasons		615 (A)
Total material price variance		615 (F)

(iii) **Reasons for the occurrence of the material price variance**

A favourable material price variance of £615 was reported for the five weeks ended 31 May 20X8. The standard price used as the basis for this calculation was out of date, however, and was too high. If a more realistic standard had been used, the actual cost was in fact greater than the standard cost, not less than the standard cost. The purchasing department had therefore purchased material at a price greater than the realistic standard (although at a price lower than the out of date standard).

The purchasing department have therefore been inefficient, not efficient.

(iv) **Implications of one scrapped barrel**

(1) **Material usage variance**

The material usage variance shows that 10 litres more than standard were used. As the standard usage per barrel is 10 litres it is possible that the scrapped barrel is the reason for this adverse variance.

(2) **Labour efficiency variance**

The labour efficiency variance shows that eight hours more than standard were worked. As a standard eight hours should be worked per barrel it is possible that the scrapped barrel is the reason for this adverse variance.

(3) **Labour rate variance**

328 hours were actually worked during the five weeks. Overtime is paid on hours in excess of 320 hours, and hence an overtime premium of eight hours x £8 = £64 was paid in the period. Suppose the eight hours of overtime were worked because one barrel was scrapped (see (2) above). The total labour rate variance is £164 and so there is still £164 - £64 = £100 of the variance not explained by the scrapping of the barrel. This £100 would be due to other, unexplained reasons.

(v) **Why the fixed overheads might not be controllable by the processing department**

(1) The apportionment of both budgeted and fixed overheads to the department is done on the arbitrary basis of budgeted machine hours. Budgeted machine hours are determined by budgeted production volume, which is outside the control of the processing department.

(2) The actual overheads apportioned to the processing department are a share of total fixed overheads. The processing department is unable to control the fixed overheads incurred in other parts of Croxton Ltd, however.

Note: Only one reason was required for (v).

PRACTICE ASSESSMENT 4
FINANCIAL PERFORMANCE

Time allowed: 2.5 hours

Section 1

Task 1.1

The following information has been calculated for one unit of product, Plate.

Each unit requires 2 litres of material at a cost of £3.50 per litre.

Each unit requires 0.5 hours of grade A labour at £15 per hour, and 0.25 hours of grade B labour at £10 per hour.

Fixed production overheads are £100,000 and budgeted output is 20,000 units.

Complete the standard cost card:

Standard cost card for per unit of Plate	
	£
Direct materials	
Direct labour – grade A	
Direct labour – grade B	
Fixed overhead	
Total standard cost per unit	

....

Task 1.2

The relationship between distribution costs (y) and output of production and sales (x) can be described by the equation:

y = a + bx

You are given the following distribution costs at two different levels of output:

Output (x)	Distribution costs (y)
1,500	14,500
3,000	19,000

(a) **Calculate the values of a and b, using the two activity levels**

	£
a	
b	

(b) **Use the values of a and b in the equation to determine the distribution costs at the following activity levels.**

Output	£
2,000 units	
4,000 units	

(c) **Complete the following sentence:**

The value of distribution costs for **2,000/4,000** units is most accurate.

....

Task 1.3

The following budgetary control report has been provided

	Budget		Actual	
Units	1,100		1,240	
Material	5,280 litres	£14,784	5,800 litres	£17,100
Labour	2,750 hours	£23,375	3,280 hours	£27,060
Fixed overheads		£4,400		£4,650
Total cost		£42,559		£48,810

The following variances have been calculated:

Fixed overhead expenditure	£250
Direct materials price	£860 A
Direct materials usage	£426
Direct labour rate	£820
Direct labour efficiency	£1,530 A
Fixed overhead volume	£560 F

Complete the operating statement:

	£	£	£
Budgeted/Standard cost for actual production			
Variances	Favourable	Adverse	
Direct materials price			
Direct materials usage			
Direct labour rate			
Direct labour efficiency			
Fixed overhead expenditure			
Fixed overhead volume			
Total variance			
Actual cost of actual production			

Task 1.4

A company has the following historic information about the cost of material.

	May 20X9	June 20X9	July 20X9
	£	£	£
Total cost	£50,000	£52,000	£55,000
Total quantity purchased	5,000 kg	5,100 kg	5,300 kg

(a) **The cost index for July 20X9 based on May 20X9 being the base period of 100 is:**

A   100

B   90.9

C   103.8

D   96.3

(b) In August 20X9, the cost index is 110 (where May 20X9 is the base period of 100).

If the total cost is £60,500, the number of kg purchased is:

A   6,050 kg

B   6,655 kg

C   5,500 kg

D   5,600 kg

Task 1.5

A business makes one product. Fixed overheads are absorbed on the basis of machine hours. The standard cost card shows that fixed overheads are to be absorbed on the basis of 3 machine hours per unit at a rate of £6 per hour. The budgeted level of production is 10,000 units.

The actual results for the period were that fixed overheads were £192,000, actual machine hours were 29,000 and the actual units produced were 9,500.

(a)   **The fixed overhead expenditure variance is:**

A   £12,000 Favourable

B   £12,000 Adverse

C   £18,000 Adverse

D   £21,000 Adverse

(b)   **The fixed overhead volume variance is:**

A   £9,000 Adverse

B   £9,000 Favourable

C   £6,000 Adverse

D   £3,000 Adverse

(c)   **The fixed overhead efficiency variance is:**

A   £3,000 Adverse

B   £6,000 Adverse

C   £6,000 Favourable

D   £9,000 Favourable

(d)   **The fixed overhead capacity variance is:**

A   £3,000 Adverse

B   £6,000 Adverse

C   £6,000 Favourable

D   £21,000 Adverse

Task 1.6

A company makes 3 products with the following standard cost information, and predicted maximum sales demand.

The material available in the coming period is 8,000 kg

The labour hours available in the coming period are 2,000 hours.

	Product		
	A	B	C
Direct materials @ £3 per kg	£9	£6	£12
Direct labour @ £12 per hour	£6	£12	£18
Selling price	£20	£30	£40
Maximum sales demand	1,000 units	800 units	600 units

Complete the table to determine the production plan which will maximise contribution.

Product	Units

....

Task 1.7

The costs of the canteen department of a manufacturing business are estimated to be £20,000 for the following quarter. Both the packaging and assembly departments use the canteen. They have 20 and 30 employees respectively, but 50% of the assembly department work nights, when the canteen is not open. The packaging department employees do not work nights.

Complete the table below to show how much canteen overhead will be apportioned to each of the packaging and assembly departments.

Overhead apportioned to packaging department	£
Overhead apportioned to assembly department	£

....

Task 1.8

The standard direct materials cost for a business's product is:

3 kg @ £15 per kg = £45.00

During the last month production was 2,600 units of the product and the actual materials cost was £149,910 for 7,890 kgs. The market price of the materials unexpectedly increased by 20% for the whole month.

Complete the following sentences:

The total materials price variance is £ [   ] adverse/favourable.

The planning element of the materials price variance that has been caused by the price increase is £ [   ] adverse/favourable.

The control element of the materials price variance caused by other factors is

£ [   ] adverse/favourable.

Section 2

Task 2.1

A company makes and sells a single product. The forecast income statement (profit and loss account) and statement of financial position (balance sheet) are shown below.

- The forecast is based on an assumed sales price of £8 per unit, and anticipated demand of 500,000 units.

	£'000
Budgeted income statement	
Revenue (Turnover)	4,000
Cost of production	
Direct materials	1,500
Direct labour	500
Fixed production overheads	800
Total cost of sales	2,800
Gross profit	**1,200**
Fixed selling and distribution costs	85
Fixed administration costs	210
Operating profit	**905**
Budgeted statement of financial position	
Non-current (fixed) assets	
Machinery	1,600
Current assets	
Inventory (stock) of raw materials	280
Receivables (debtors)	800
Current liabilities	
Payables (creditors)	(150)
Net current assets	**930**
Long-term loans	500
Net assets	**2,030**
Represented by:	
Share capital and reserves	2,030
Net assets	**2,030**

Draft a report to the finance director which

(a) includes calculations of the performance indicators listed below

    (i)   gross profit margin

    (ii)   operating profit margin

    (iii) direct materials as a percentage of revenue

    (iv) direct materials cost per unit

    (v)   return on net assets

    (vi) inventory turnover in days

    (vii) receivables' collection period in days

    (viii) gearing

(b) Advises on the following scenarios:

    (i)   The gross profit margin for the industry is 35%. Advise the finance director, what the selling price would have to be if demand and costs stay the same, in order to achieve this margin.

    (ii)   The operating profit margin for the industry is 25%. If it is not possible to change the selling price, demand or most costs, but it may be possible to reduce fixed administration costs, what would the percentage reduction in fixed administration costs have to be, in order to achieve a gross profit margin of 25%?

    (iii) The average receivables' payment period in the industry is 65 days. If sales are unchanged, advise the finance director by how much (in £) the year-end receivables would have to change, to achieve the industry average payment period.

    To: Finance Director

    Subject: Key performance indicators

    From: Accounting Technician

    Date: 26 October 20X2

Gross profit margin – selling price to achieve industry margin

Operating profit margin – percentage reduction in administration costs

Receivables' collection period – change to achieve industry average

Appendix

	£
Gross profit margin	
Operating profit margin	
Direct materials as a percentage of revenue	
Direct materials cost per unit	
Return on net assets	
Inventory turnover in days	
Receivables' collection period in days	
Gearing	

· ·

Task 2.2

Rix Limited manufactures one standard product. Rix Limited operates a standard costing system.

Data from the budget and the standard product cost for the last month are given below.

1   Budgeted and standard cost data:

Budgeted sales and production for the month 10,500 units

Standard cost for each unit of product:

Direct material:	A	4 kilograms	@ £2.50 per kilogram
	B	6 kilograms	@ £1 per kilogram
Labour:		0.5 hours	@ £16 per hour

Fixed production overhead is absorbed @ 300% of direct wages.

2   Actual data for last month:

Production and sales were 11,000 units sold at standard price.

Direct materials consumed:

A 45,000 kilograms, costing £108,000

B 62,000 kilograms, costing £68,200

Direct wages incurred 5,250 hours and cost £94,500.

Fixed production overhead incurred £250,000

Tasks

Prepare a report to the finance director, which includes an operating statement reconciling the standard absorption cost of actual production to actual costs for last months, and explain what the fixed overhead variances reveal about last month's production, and the success of the manager responsible for overhead costs.

Report

To: A Finance Director

From: An Accountant

Date: 14 April 20X2

Subject: Last month's variances

I enclose (in the appendix) an operating statement reconciling the standard cost of actual production last month to the actual cost.

Fixed overhead variances

Appendix

Reconciliation statement – previous month			
			£
	£	£	£
Standard absorption cost of actual production			
	(F)	(A)	
Variances			
Material A price			
Material A usage			
Material B price			
Material B usage			
Labour rate			
Labour efficiency			
Fixed overhead expenditure			
Fixed overhead efficiency			
Fixed overhead capacity			
Actual absorption cost of actual production			

PRACTICE ASSESSMENT 4
FINANCIAL PERFORMANCE

ANSWERS

Section 1

Task 1.1

Standard cost card for per unit of Plate	
	£
Direct materials (2 x £3.50)	7.00
Direct labour – grade A (0.5 x £15)	7.50
Direct labour – grade B (0.25 x £10)	2.50
Fixed overhead (£100,000/20,000)	5.00
Total standard cost per unit	22.00

Task 1.2

(a)

	£
a	10,000
b	3

Workings

Substituting the outputs and corresponding distribution costs into the equation gives:

£14,500 = a + 1,500 b

£19,000 = a + 3,000 b

Subtracting the two equations gives:

£4,500 = 1,500 b

b = £3 per unit

Substituting this into the first equation gives:

£14,500 = a + 1,500 x £3

a = £10,000

(b)

Output	£
2,000 units (£10,000 + £3 x 2,000)	16,000
4,000 units (£10,000 + £3 x 4,000)	22,000

(c)   The value of distribution costs for **2,000** units is most accurate.

Tutorial note – this is because this is within the range of the activities (1,500 – 3,000) which were used to determine a and b in the equation (interpolation). 4,000 units is an activity outside the range (and so requires extrapolation).

Task 1.3

	£	£	£
Budgeted/Standard cost for actual production			47,976
Variances	Favourable	Adverse	
Direct materials price		860	
Direct materials usage	426		
Direct labour rate	820		
Direct labour efficiency		1,530	
Fixed overhead expenditure		250	
Fixed overhead volume	560		
Total variance	1,806 F	2,640 A	834 A
Actual cost of actual production			48,810

Workings

Standard cost of actual production.

Budgeted cost per unit = £42,559/1,100 = £38.69 per unit

Budgeted cost of 1,240 units = £38.69 x 1,240 = £47,976

Fixed overhead expenditure variance – actual overheads larger than budgeted, therefore expenditure variance is adverse.

Direct materials usage variance – budgeted usage = 5,280/1,100 = 4.8 litres/unit

Actual usage = 5,800/1,240 =4.68 litres/unit ie lower usage than budgeted so favourable.

Labour rate variance – budgeted rate = £23,375/2,750 = £8.50 per hour

Actual rate = £27,060/3,280 = £8.25 per hour ie lower rate than budgeted, so favourable.

Task 1.4

(a)   The cost index for July 20X9 based on May 20X9 being the base period of 100 is:

   C   103.8

Working

Cost per kg for May = £50,000/5,000kg = £10 per kg

Cost per kg for July = £55,000/5,300kg = £10.38 per kg

Therefore July's index = £10.38/£10 x 100 = 103.8

(b)   In August 20X9, the cost index is 110 (where May 20X9 is the base period of 100). If the total cost is £60,500, the number of kg purchased is

   C   5,500 kg

Working

Cost per kg in May is £10 per kg

So cost in August = £10/100 x 110 = £11 per kg

Therefore, number of kg purchased = £60,500/£11 = 5,500 kg.

Task 1.5

(a)   B

(b)   A

(c)   A

(d)   B

Workings

Fixed overhead expenditure variance

	£
Budgeted fixed overhead 10,000 units × 3 hours × £6	180,000
Actual fixed overhead	192,000
Expenditure variance	12,000 (A)

Fixed overhead volume variance

	£
Standard hours for actual production @ standard OAR 9,500 units × 3 hours × £6	171,000
Standard hours for budgeted production @ standard OAR 10,000 units × 3 hours × £6	180,000
Volume variance	9,000 (A)

Fixed overhead efficiency variance

	£
Standard hours for actual production @ standard OAR 9,500 × 3 hours × £6	171,000
Actual hours @ standard OAR 29,000 × £6	174,000
Efficiency variance	3,000 (A)

Fixed overhead capacity variance

	£
Actual hours @ standard OAR 29,000 × £6	174,000
Budgeted hours @ standard OAR 10,000 × 3 × £6	180,000
Capacity variance	6,000 (A)

Task 1.6

Product	Units
A	1,000
B	800
C	466

Workings

1   Determine the limiting factor

Material usage per unit of each product:

A   £9/£3 = 3 kg per unit

B   £6/£3 = 2 kg per unit

C   £12/£3 = 4 kg per unit

So maximum sales demand would use:

A   3 kg x 1,000 = 3,000 kg

B   2 kg x 800 = 1,600 kg

C   4 kg x 600 = 2,400 kg

Therefore total materials usage for this demand = 3,000 + 1,600 + 2,400 = 7,000 kg

8,000 kg are available so material is not the limiting factor

Labour hours per unit of each product:

A   £6/£12 = 0.5 hours per unit

B   £12/£12 = 1 hour per unit

C   £18/£12 = 1.5 hours per unit

So maximum sales demand would require:

A   0.5 x 1,000 = 500 hours

B   1 x 800 = 800 hours

C   1.5 x 600 = 900 hours

Therefore, total labour hours for this demand = 500 + 800 + 900 = 2,200 hours

Only 2,000 hours are available so labour hours is a limiting factor.

2   **Contribution per limiting factor:**

A   (£20 - £9 - £6)/0.5 = £10 per labour hour

B   (£30 - £12 - £6)/1 = £12 per labour hour

C   (£40 - £12 - £18)/1.5 = £6.67 per labour hour

Therefore, rank B, A and then C.

3   **Production to maximise contribution**

B 800 units use 800 hours

A   1,000 units use 500 hours, so 1,300 hours used so far

C   Remaining 2,000 – 1,300 = 700 hours can be used for product C. Makes 700/1.5 = 466 units.

··

Task 1.7

Overhead apportioned to packaging department	£11,429
Overhead apportioned to assembly department	£8,571

Workings

Number of employees who use canteen = 20 + 50% x 30 = 35 employees

Cost per employee = £20,000/35 = £571.43 per employee

Therefore cost apportioned to packaging department = 20 x £571.43 = £11,429

Cost apportioned to assembly department = 15 x £571.43 = £8,571

··

Task 1.8

The total materials price variance is £31,560 Adverse.

The planning element of the materials price variance that has been caused by the price increase is £23,670 Adverse.

The control element of the materials price variance caused by other factors is £7,890 Adverse.

Workings

Total materials price variance

	£
Standard cost for actual quantity 7,890 x £15	118,350
Actual cost	149,910
	31,560 (A)

Planning variance caused by price increase

	£
Standard cost for actual quantity 7,890 x £15	118,350
Adjusted cost for actual quantity 7,890 x £18*	142,020
	23,670 (A)

*Adjusted price is 120% of £15 = £18

Control variance caused by other factors

	£
Adjusted cost for actual quantity 7,890 x £18	142,020
Actual cost	149,910
	7,890 (A)

Section 2

Task 2.1

(a)

Gross profit margin	30%
Operating profit margin	22.63%
Direct materials as a percentage of turnover	37.5%
Direct materials cost per unit	£3 per unit
Return on net assets	44.58%
Inventory turnover in days	36.5 days
Receivables' collection period in days	73 days
Gearing	0.25

Workings

Gross profit $= \dfrac{£1,200,000}{£4,000,000} \times 100 = 30\%$

Operating profit margin $= \dfrac{£905,000}{£4,000,000} \times 100 = 22.63\%$

Direct materials as a percentage of turnover $= \dfrac{£1,500,000}{£4,000,000} \times 100 = 37.5\%$

Direct materials cost per unit $= \dfrac{£1,500,000}{500,000} = £3$ per unit

Return on net assets $= \dfrac{£905,000}{£2,030,000} \times 100 = 44.58\%$

Inventory turnover in days $= \dfrac{£280,000}{£2,800,000} \times 365 = 36.5$ days

Receivables' collection period in days $= \dfrac{£800,000}{£4,000,000} \times 365 = 73$ days

Gearing = long term loans/(share capital + reserves) $= \dfrac{£500,000}{£2,030,000} = 0.25$

(Note that long term loans/(long term loans + share capital + reserves)would be an acceptable answer here = 0.20).

(b)

To:	Finance Director
Subject:	Key performance indicators
From:	Accounting Technician
Date:	26 October 20X2

(i) **Gross profit margin – selling price to achieve industry margin**

The current gross profit margin is 30% but the industry margin is 35%. Therefore, for the same level of costs, the sales price would have to increase to £8.62 per unit.

(ii) **Operating profit margin – percentage reduction in administration costs**

For an operating profit margin of 25% when the only cost/revenue that can change is administration costs, these would have to decrease by 45.24%

(iii) **Receivables' collection period – change to achieve industry average**

Receivables would have to reduce by £87,671 to achieve the industry average of receivables' days of 65, for this level of revenue.

Workings

(i) Gross profit margin of 35%

Cost of sales = £2,800,000

Revenue would have to be £2,800,000/65% = £4,307,692

Sales price per unit would have to be £4,307,692/500,000 = £8.62

(ii) Operating profit margin of 25%

Operating profit/revenue = 25%

Revenue would be unchanged, so operating profit would be 25% x £4,000,000 = £1,000,000 ie an increase of £95,000.

Therefore, fixed administration overheads would have to decrease by £95,000.

Percentage reduction in fixed administration overheads = £95,000/£210,000 = 45.24%

(iii) Industry receivables' days are 65 days

Revenue x 65/365 = receivables

£4,000,000 x 65/365 = £712,329

Reduction in receivables = £800,000 - £712,329 = £87,671

Task 2.2

Report

To: A Finance Director

From: An Accountant

Date: 14 April 20X2

Subject: Last month's variances

I enclose (in the appendix) an operating statement reconciling the standard cost of actual production last month to the actual cost.

Fixed overhead variances

The total fixed overhead variance is a favourable variance £14,000. £14,000 more fixed overheads were absorbed than were actually incurred.

Only £2,000 of this favourable variance is due to the actual fixed overheads being lower than the budgeted fixed overheads (this difference is the fixed overhead expenditure variance). Therefore, a manager responsible for incurring fixed overheads, can only be credited with a saving of £2,000.

The remaining £12,000 variance is caused by the volume of units produced being greater than expected. The volume was greater entirely because of increased efficiency of labour – more units (11,000) were produced in the labour hours available (5,520) than were expected (10,500).

None of the favourable variance was due to the company having greater capacity than expected (nil capacity variance) as the actual hours worked were equal to those budgeted.

Appendix

Reconciliation Statement for last month

	£	£	£
Budgeted cost (W)			528,000
Cost variances	F	A	
Material A price	4,500		
Material A usage		2,500	
Material B price		6,200	
Material B usage	4,000		
Direct wages rate		10,500	
Direct wages efficiency	4,000		
Fixed overhead expenditure	2,000		
Fixed overhead efficiency	12,000		
Fixed overhead capacity	0		
	26,500	19,200	7,300 F
Actual cost (£108,000 + £68,200 + £94,500 + £250,000)			520,700

Workings

Standard absorption cost per unit

			£	£
Direct material A	4 kgs	@	2.50	10.00
Direct material B	6 kgs	@	1.00	6.00
Labour	0.5 hrs	@	16.00	8.00
Fixed overhead	300% of direct labour			24.00
Total standard cost				48.00

Therefore, standard cost for actual production = 11,000 x £48 = £528,000

Cost variances

Material A price variance

	£
Actual usage at standard price	
45,000 × £2.50	112,500
Actual cost	108,000
	4,500 Fav

Material A usage variance

   Standard usage for actual production at standard cost

      11,000 × 4 kg × £2.50   110,000

   Actual usage at standard cost

      45,000 × £2.50   112,500

                                           2,500 Adv

Material B price variance

   Actual usage at standard price   £

      62,000 × £1   62,000

   Actual cost   68,200

                                           6,200 Adv

Material B usage variance

   Standard usage for actual production at standard cost

      11,000 × 6 kg × £1   66,000

   Actual usage at standard cost

      62,000 × £1   62,000

                                         4,000 Fav

Labour rate variance

   Actual hours at standard rate

      5,250 × £16   84,000

   Actual hours at actual rate   94,500

                                     10,500 Adv

Labour efficiency variance

   Standard hours for actual production at standard rate

      11,000 × 0.5 × £16   88,000

   Actual hours at standard rate

      5,250 × £16   84,000

                                         4,000 Fav

      Fixed overhead expenditure variance   £

      Budgeted fixed overhead (£24 x 10,500)   252,000

      Actual fixed overhead   250,000

                                         2,000 Fav

Fixed overhead efficiency variance

Standard hours for actual production at standard absorption rate

11,000 × 0.5 x £48*	264,000

Actual hours at standard absorption rate

5,250 × £48	252,000
	12,000 Fav

*£24 per unit is absorbed, or £24/0.5 = £48 per labour hour

Fixed overhead capacity variance

Actual hours at standard absorption rate

5,250 × £48	252,000

Budgeted hours at standard absorption rate

10,500 x 0.5 x £48	252,000
	0

Notes

Notes

Notes

Notes

Notes